CAPTAIN OF SALVATION

SUPERIORITY OF JESUS

LESLIE M. JOHN

CAPTAIN OF SALVATION

SUPERIORITY OF JESUS

LESLIE M. JOHN

The entire text of this book and graphics are deposited with Library of Congress Copyright Office, 101 Independence Avenue, SE Washington, DC 20559-6000, USA. This work is protected by Law in US; and internationally, according to The Berne Convention 1971

ISBN-13: 978-0-9907801-9-9
ISBN-10: 0-9907801-9-8

PREFACE

For God so loved the world, that he gave his only begotten Son, that whosoever believeth in him should not perish, but have everlasting life. For God sent not his Son into the world to condemn the world; but that the world through him might be saved. (John 3:16-17)

Lord Jesus Christ is the Son of God and He said He and the Father are one. No one comes to Him unless the Father draws one to the Lord. Jesus Christ is the creator and not a created being. He is superior to the entire creation.

"For by him were all things created, that are in heaven, and that are in earth, visible and invisible, whether they be thrones, or dominions, or principalities, or powers: all things were created by him, and for him: And he is before all things, and by him all things consist. And he is the head of the body, the church: who is the beginning, the firstborn from the dead; that in all things he might have the preeminence" (Colossians 1:16-18)

This book presents sublime theme of man's redemption from sin and everlasting life. Man rebelled against God by transgressing His command.

The only way available for reconciling man with God was by the substitutionary death of the Lord Jesus Christ and by His resurrection. Whoever believes in Him will not perish but will have everlasting life.

Bible says: "For all have sinned, and come short of the glory of God" (Romans 3:23)

"For the wages of sin is death; but the gift of God is eternal life through Jesus Christ our Lord" (Romans 6:23)

"If we say that we have no sin, we deceive ourselves, and the truth is not in us" (1 John 1:8)

"That if thou shalt confess with thy mouth the Lord Jesus, and shalt believe in thine heart that God hath raised him from the dead, thou shalt be saved. For with the heart man believeth unto righteousness; and with the mouth confession is made unto salvation" (Romans 10:9-10)

INTRODUCTION

WHAT SALVATION IS IT?

SALVTION is the act of saving or preservation from destruction. When it comes to refer man's salvation it means redemption of man from the bondage of sin. It is the redemption from the liability of eternal damnation. It is the redemption from being cast into the "lake of fire'.

- And shall cast them into a furnace of fire: there shall be wailing and gnashing of teeth. (Matthew 13:42)
- Being justified freely by his grace through the redemption that is in Christ Jesus: (Romans 3:24)
- For when we were yet without strength, in due time Christ died for the ungodly. (Romans 5:6)

THE MYSTERY REVEALED

"If you have heard of the dispensation of the grace of God which is given me toward you" (Ephesians 3:2)

Apostle Paul humbly acknowledges in Ephesians Chapter 3 that he was a prisoner of Jesus Christ to be the minister for Gentiles. He revealed the mystery of the dispensation of grace of God and said that this mystery was made known to the Apostles and the prophets by the Holy Spirit.

It was about the equal inheritance of the heavenly blessings by Gentiles on par with the Jews who accept Jesus as their Lord and also to be the partakers of God's promises and to become the members of the body of Christ.

Paul was made minister of the gospel of Jesus Christ unto the Gentiles according to the gift of grace of God that was given to him for his effectual work for God (cf. Acts Ch.9:15 and Eph. Ch.3:6-8). He humbled himself to the extent of saying that he was less than the least of all the saints and yet this privilege to preach the gospel to the Gentiles was given to him.

He considered preaching to the Gentiles and revealing God's purposes was a privilege given to him and such preaching was the result of abundant grace of God towards him. He wrote that it was with that purpose he revealed to the Gentiles the unsearchable riches of Christ and to make everyone see the plan of God.

This mystery was hidden in God who created all things by Jesus Christ. This mystery was hidden not only during the Old Testament period but even unto the time when Apostle Paul himself declared that God purposed that the Gentiles should be on par with Jews and reap heavenly blessings.

CONTENTS

CHAPTER 1
CAPTAIN OF SALVATION

"For it became him, for whom are all things, and by whom are all things, in bringing many sons unto glory, to make the captain of their salvation perfect through sufferings" (Hebrews 2:10)

Hebrews 2:10 has three points in it.

- Firstly, it shows who is that who orders things out,
- Secondly, who executed the things, and whose sake all things are ordered out,
- Thirdly, it eventually points to those who are benefited of such action.

For carrying out any work there needs to be someone who first writes an order and then there needs to be someone who executes it. Someone who writes an order has to be one that has authority to write such an order else it is tantamount to a mere worthless writing; and likewise, someone who executes the order has to be one who is competent to do such work else it would end up in shambles. We cannot afford to do things at random with unauthorized people writing an order and incapable ones executing it.

If earthly things had to be done so meticulously with planning then how great care must have been taken by the one who made heaven and earth, and created man to live therein. Science has never proved rightly until now that big-bang theory was right.

Man's disobedience of God's word and God's plan of salvation for man are not mere plans of trivial importance to be viewed negligently. If such a metaphor such as rolling in the grave is true, it could be Darwin, who would be rolling in his grave repenting for having created so much confusion about evolution. God is the creator and He has the ultimate authority to have His own way of offering salvation for mankind. Lord Jesus Christ is the Captain of our salvation.

When Job faced with trials and tribulations he questioned God, but when God turned to him and asked Him questions, Job laid his hands on his mouth and had no answers to God.

Someone once questioned as to how Jesus could a die substitutionary death on behalf of another, and wondered if the blood Jesus was a detergent to wash the sins of a sinner? That is the way unregenerate man thinks of the blood of Jesus and His sacrifice.

Would it not have been possible for God to have another plan of salvation, say by just blowing His breath into the air and order salvation to sinner? Surely it would have been possible if God thought it is the right way of doing things; it is within God's sovereign plan and power as to which method He was to use.

However, when it comes to the creator showing His utmost love towards His creation that was not a method, or any other method than offering His only begotten Son that God thought of.

The scriptures and the science both alike say that the life is in blood. Then, it was the life that God thought of offering for fallen man's sake. He died in order that we may live. He rose in order that we may also rise from the dead and live in Him.

It pleased God to shed that precious blood of His only Son for the salvation of mankind. It is a great token of love that God has shown that the blood of Jesus had the efficacy of cleansing the sins of sinner. Lord Jesus is the express image of invisible God, and by Him were all things created, and everything that was created was created for Him, and in Him all things consist.

"Who is the image of the invisible God, the firstborn of every creature: For by him were all things created, that are in heaven, and that are in earth, visible and invisible, whether they be thrones, or dominions, or principalities, or powers: all things were created by him, and for him: And he is before all things, and by him all things consist" (Colossians 1:15-17)

To a question posed by a learned Nicodemus, a man of the Pharisees, a ruler of the Jews, as to how a man can be born again, and was it by entering into the mother's womb second time that a man is born again, Jesus said "except a man be born of water and Spirit, he cannot enter into the kingdom of God". The Lord said, that which is born of the flesh is of flesh and that which is born of the Spirit is spirit. (cf. John 3:1-6)

Jesus had a reply to Nicodemus, who asked how these things could be and the answer from Jesus was...

"If I have told you earthly things, and ye believe not, how shall ye believe, if I tell you of heavenly things?" (John 3:12)

For such as those who make insulting remarks as to whether the blood of Jesus is detergent to cleanse the sins of a sinner, Apostle Paul has something to say and it is...

"For the preaching of the cross is to them that perish foolishness; but unto us which are saved it is the power of God" (1 Corinthians 1:18)

"But the natural man receiveth not the things of the Spirit of God: for they are foolishness unto him: neither can he know them, because they are spiritually discerned" (1 Corinthians 2:14)

It is not the clothes that we wear that need to be cleansed or the physical body that needs to be cleansed to have everlasting life but it the inner man; the soul of man that needs be cleansed and presented as righteous before God, and that is possible only by the cleansing of sins by the power of the precious blood of Lord Jesus Christ. It is the only one way available for salvation.

If a man chooses to be cleansed of his clothes and physical body, detergent or soap is enough, and his body perishes as the LORD said, "dust thou art, and unto dust shalt thou return".

It is true that every man's physical body will return to dust, but the believer's soul will be with the Lord forever and ever, while the unbeliever's soul will eternally suffer when it is cast into the 'lake of fire' by God.

Lord Jesus Christ, who is the Way, the Truth, and the Life, is the author and commander of the salvation, and there is no other way whereby anyone could be saved.

"Neither is there salvation in any other: for there is none other name under heaven given among men, whereby we must be saved". (Acts 4:12)

CHAPTER 2
SUPERIORITY OF JESUS

GOD SPOKE IN DIVERSE MANNERS

"God, who at sundry times and in divers manners spake in time past unto the fathers by the prophets, Hath in these last days spoken unto us by his Son, whom he hath appointed heir of all things, by whom also he made the worlds" (Hebrews 1:1-2)

Bible says God spoke to the children of Israel by the mouth of the Prophets in the Old Testament period. The LORD sent His only son Jesus, who in His incarnation, lived among men and He spoke the Word of the Father to all. The Father appointed Jesus, His only Son, as heir of all things, by whom also the LORD made the worlds.

The writer emphasizes the veracity of the Word of the LORD to Jews, who were converted to Christianity, that the words of Lord Jesus are superior over Mosaic Law.

Old Testament sacrifices are no more needed, because Jesus died on our behalf, as sacrifice once and for all. The writer wrote these words in order to see that those who found the truth may not defect to Judaism.

The Writer specifically points to the superiority of Jesus and His nature, and His deity even though He was fully man in this world.

Not every Prophet had similar revelation or full revelation of God and His word, but to each one was given little and God spoke to each one in different methods.

To Noah God showed the world that would be destroyed and the salvation to him and his family; to Abraham God showed a Nation that He was going to choose for Himself, and call the people of that Nation as His people; to Jacob He gave the name of that Nation, and showed the tribe from which He would come as a Lion to judge the world; to David, and Isaiah He showed the lineage from which He would come; to Daniel He showed the end times; to Micah He showed His nativity, to Malachi He showed His forerunner, who was John the Baptist.

The LORD spoke to Moses from the burning bush, He spoke to Elijah in a still voice. He spoke through Lord Jesus Christ, His only begotten Son, in the last days.

JESUS THE IMPRINT OF GOD

Who being the brightness of his glory, and the express image of his person, and upholding all things by the word of his power, when he had by himself purged our sins, sat down on the right hand of the Majesty on high; (Hebrews 1:3)

Lord Jesus Christ is the radiance and express imprint of the Father. He upholds all things by the word of His power, and after He offered Himself as sacrifice for the sins of the world, sat down on the right hand of the Majesty on High.

While the Lord offered His blood as propitiation, salvation is available only to those who confess by mouth that He is the Lord, and believe in heart that God raised Him from the death on the third day.

Mark the Gospel writer writes that the Lord was received up into heaven, and sat on the right hand of God.

Luke the Gospel writer, a physician, a companion of Apostle Paul writes that the 'Son of man' sits on the right hand of God.

Apostle Paul, although not named as writer of the Book of Hebrews, yet going by the style of writing he is believed to be the writer. He says that through the eternal Spirit offered Himself without spot to God. He purges our conscience from dead works to serve the living God (Cf. 2 Corinthians 4:4, Mark 16:19, Luke 22:69)

HIS EXCELLENT NAME

"Being made so much better than the angels, as he hath by inheritance obtained a more excellent name than they. For unto which of the angels said he at any time, Thou art my Son, this day have I begotten thee? And again, I will be to him a Father, and he shall be to me a Son?" (Hebrews 1:4-5)

In dignity and in office Lord Jesus Christ (who is not an angel) is superior to angels. The contrast is made to better understand Lord Jesus. Angels do not accept worship from humans, but Jesus having been appointed by the Father heir of all things, is alone who deserves worship.

When John bowed down to angel the latter is said he is a fellow servant and did not accept worship. In the last days (in the context it means during Messianic days) God spoke to us by his Son, Lord Jesus Christ, who, by sacrifice of himself on our behalf has inherited an excellent name above all names that at the name of Jesus every knee, of that which is heaven, and that which are in earth and that which are under the heaven, will bow down, and confess that He is Lord to the glory of the Father.

God is still speaking to us through His word, and in our quiet times when we seek His guidance through sincere prayer. In His incarnation, he was made little lower than angels (Hebrews 2:7, Psalm 8:5, and Philippians 2:6-8). He and the Father are one (John 10:30).

The Lord is now seated on the right hand of the Majesty and pleading on our behalf. Angels and authorities and all powers have been made subject to Him.

"And the Word was made flesh, and dwelt among us, (and we beheld his glory, the glory as of the only begotten of the Father,) full of grace and truth" (John 1:14).

(cf. Philippians 2:9-11, 1 Peter 3:22, Revelation 22:9, Hebrews 2:7, Ephesians 1:21, Colossians 2:10)

JESUS IS SUPERIOR TO ANGELS

"And again, when he bringeth in the first-begotten into the world, he saith, And let all the angels of God worship him. And of the angels he saith, Who maketh his angels spirits, and his ministers a flame of fire. But unto the Son he saith, Thy throne, O God, is for ever and ever: a sceptre of righteousness is the sceptre of thy kingdom" (Hebrews 1:6-8)

Some teach that Jesus was 'Michael' the angel; but this is heretical teaching inasmuch as He was never an angel nor is an angel, but He was and is the 'Son of God'. He was not a messenger from the Father, but He was the message.

The title 'Son of God' belongs to Him and Him alone because of the sacrifice he rendered of His own flesh and blood for the sake of salvation of mankind. That is the reason He was called the first-begotten Son and angels are commanded to worship Him.

The Father blessed Him saying His throne is established forever and ever, and He being equal with the Father, is also called God. His scepter of righteousness is His kingdom. He was and is our perfect redeemer, therefore, He was said to be so much better than angels.

Paul writes in Colossians 2:18 to be careful of those who beguile us with rewards of worshipping angels and admonishes not to get puffed up in fleshly mind. The scriptures prove that Jesus is superior to angels. (cf. Psalm 2:7, 2 Samuel 7:14)",

JESUS IS GOD: HE IS LORD

"Thou hast loved righteousness, and hated iniquity; therefore God, even thy God, hath anointed thee with the oil of gladness above thy fellows. (Hebrews 1:9)

Hebrews 1:9 does not point to King Solomon but to Jesus, who is God. The Father God has anointed Him with the oil of gladness above all His fellows. Similar to a Governor addressing another Governor as "Governor", the Father God calls the Son as 'God', and if so, the testimony of whom else can be considered as greater than His? By the inspiration of Holy Spirit John the Gospel writer testifies in John 1:1 that the Word was with God and the Word was God (cf. John 20:28, Titus 2:13, Leviticus 8:12, Luke 4:18).

In power and office the Jehovah made Jesus the 'King of kings', and 'Lord of lords'.

Jesus said "I and my Father are one" (John 10:30)

"These shall make war with the Lamb, and the Lamb shall overcome them: for he is Lord of lords, and King of kings: and they that are with him are called, and chosen, and faithful". (Revelation 17:14)

"And he hath on his vesture and on his thigh a name written, KING OF KINGS, AND LORD OF LORDS" (Revelation 19:16)

"And he is the head of the body, the church: who is the beginning, the firstborn from the dead; that in all things he might have the preeminence" (Colossians 1:18)

"Thou lovest righteousness, and hatest wickedness: therefore God, thy God, hath anointed thee with the oil of gladness above thy fellows" (Psalms 45:7)

"Therefore we ought to give the more earnest heed to the things which we have heard, lest at any time we should let them slip" (Hebrews 2:1)

Hebrews chapter 2 verse 1 starts with the word "Therefore". That is to say that there was, in the previous chapter, a very relevant subject on which the verses in this chapter are constructed.

Indeed, it was seen that there was considerable proof provided in chapter 1 of the superiority of Jesus over the angels. If so, then we ought to give more earnest heed to the things that we heard.

In addition to what Hebrews says about Jesus, who is superior to angels, and every human being, John the Baptist, who was forerunner of Jesus (not the Gospel writer John) bears witness of Jesus and says that of Him did He spoke that He who comes after him was preferred before Him, because He was before

John, and of His fulness we all received grace for grace. He continues saying that the Law was given by Moses, but the grace and truth came by Lord Jesus. He says that no man has seen God at any time, but the only begotten Son, Lord Jesus Christ, who was in the bosom of the Father, declared Him. (cf. John 1:15-18, John 1:29)

Next day, John the Baptist says that Jesus was the Lamb of God, who takes away the sin of the world. Lord Jesus says…

"All things are delivered unto me of my Father: and no man knoweth the Son, but the Father; neither knoweth any man the Father, save the Son, and he to whomsoever the Son will reveal him. Come unto me, all ye that labour and are heavy laden and I will give you rest". (Matthew 11:27-28)

JESUS IS THE CREATOR

And, Thou, Lord, in the beginning hast laid the foundation of the earth; and the heavens are the works of thine hands: They shall perish; but thou remainest; and they all shall wax old as doth a garment; (Hebrews 1:10-11)

Lord Jesus was the Word and He was with the God, and He was God. He created heavens and the earth in the beginning. He laid the foundation of the earth, and the heavens are the work of His hands. He called forth, and they came into existence. By His word He made all things and there was nothing made without His word.

However, this sinful world, which was won by Satan, by cheating Adam and Eve, will one day perish, but the Lord will endure and He is eternal. So are we the believers, who believe in Him, will have everlasting life in Him. All this corrupted earth, will axe like old garment, and the Lorde will change every creation of these days like changing vesture.

Lord Jesus is same yesterday, today and will remain the same tomorrow. Jehovah called His name as "I am that I am"; all the time He is in present times. He was the Son born and yet He was the Father. This is a great mystery. One of the titles, for Jesus, Isiah 9:6 was "... The everlasting Father..." (Isaiah 9:6)

He is eternal and of years there shall not be an end. He reigns and the let the multitudes of isles are glad in Him. His throne is of righteousness and righteous judgment. His enemies are burned up in fire with the fire that goes from His throne. His light enlightened the world and everyone on earth saw it and trembled.

The heavens declare His righteousness and glory. The Lord creates new heavens and new earth and the former shall not be remembered.

"Rejoice in the LORD, ye righteous; and give thanks at the remembrance of his holiness". (Psalms 97:12)

"For, behold, I create new heavens and a new earth: and the former shall not be remembered, nor come into mind". (Isaiah 65:17)

(cf. Genesis 1:1, Psalms 97:1-6, Psalms 102:25-27, John 1:1)

JESUS IS DIVINE AND HUMAN

"But to which of the angels said he at any time, Sit on my right hand, until I make thine enemies thy footstool? Are they not all ministering spirits, sent forth to minister for them who shall be heirs of salvation?" (Hebrews 1:13-14)

Man in his finite knowledge, without considering that Jesus is Divine, thinks that man and woman conjugation is necessary for a child to be born; and of course it is true in the case of humans, but Lord Jesus was not a man to be born to human beings. God is Spirit and Lord Jesus was divine born of the Holy Virgin Mary, who was overshadowed by the Holy Spirit in this world in the likeness of man becoming flesh our sake.

Mark the Gospel writer emphasizes on his human nature and calls him as "Son of man", while John the Gospel writer calls Him the "Son of God".

Indeed, He had two natures, one of divine and another of human. He was fully divine and fully human.   In like manner man would like to understand the facts one contrasting with another. Therefore, the writer of Hebrews contrasts Jesus with angels, Joseph, and Moses, High Priests of Old Testament period, Prophets etc. In all comparisons and contrasts Lord Jesus is found to be the superior.

The writer argues as to which of the angels were given the privilege of being seated at Father's right hand, until the LORD the Almighty Jehovah makes all the enemies of Lord Jesus Christ to come to His footstool.

Angels are ministering spirits sent forth to minister those who are going to have eternal life and become heirs of salvation. Obviously the heirs who are going to have inheritance and to be comforted to the image of Lord Jesus Christ are those, who confess by mouth Him as the Lord, and believe in heart that God raised Him from the dead on the third day. (cf. Romans 10:9)

CHAPTER 3
HE WAS OBEDIENT

"Though he were a Son, yet learned he obedience by the things which he suffered; And being made perfect, he became the author of eternal salvation unto all them that obey him" (Hebrews 5:8-9)

Our Lord Jesus Christ practically showed what obedience is like when He died in our stead, and suffered humiliation by death on the cross, because it pleased the Father to bruise Him for our sake; thus He became the author of our eternal salvation.

The Lord desires that we should learn and show practically the obedience to the Lord's commandments to love God "with all thy heart, and with all thy soul, and with all thy mind" and to "love thy neighbour as thyself" (Ref. Matthew 22:37-38)

The children of Israel rejected "Theocracy", a direct rule by God, through His servant Moses, when He redeemed them out of slavery from Egypt, provided food for them in the wilderness, protection by day and night, and protection from their enemies.

The LORD then raised judges to rule over them, and they rejected them as well and chose to have a king over them just as nations had. Samuel the prophet warned them that the king would take their male children to fight wars and female children to work in bakeries, and yet they insisted on having a king over them.

The LORD granted their desire reluctantly; and chose Saul, a good-looking, handsome, nicely built in physique from the tribe of Benjamin to be anointed as king over them.

The LORD sent His word through Samuel the prophet and said to Saul that he should go and fight Amalekites to their utter destruction, even their infants, male or female, their sheep, oxen, etc. The LORD was against Amalekites because they were the first nation to attack innocent children of Israel from behind when they came out the land of Egypt.

In Scriptures, Amalekites are a type of 'flesh', inasmuch as they are the descendants of concubine of Eliphaz, son of Esau, who himself was carnal and sold his birthright for a "red pottage". In the New Testament Lord Jesus and Apostle Paul instructed us that we should utterly destroy our fleshly desires and carnal nature.

Saul gathered two hundred thousand footmen and ten thousand men of Judah and went out, and he did well to spare Kenites, who did good to the children of Israel when they came out of Egypt, but he disobeyed the command of the LORD by sparing Agag, king of Amalekites, and their best of sheep and oxen.

Samuel came to know about it and came to meet Saul, but then Saul had gone away from Carmel to Gilgal. Samuel travelled to Gilgal and met Saul, who lied to the prophet saying he fulfilled the command of the LORD. Then Samuel questioned him as to what was that bleating sound of sheep and lowing of the oxen that he was hearing.

CHAPTER 4
IDENTIFIED AS BROTHER

"For both he that sanctifieth and they who are sanctified are all of one: for which cause he is not ashamed to call them brethren" (Hebrews 2:11)

Not as a family member of one human family, but of the nature and the likeness of man that Jesus had on this earth that He identified as brother to those who believed in Him.

Jesus remains sanctified in eternity as the Son of God. He was set apart for a specific purpose and that was to come down to this earth in the likeness of man and dwell among men and become a sacrifice shedding His precious blood for the sake of redemption of mankind from sin that whoever believes in Him shall not perish but have everlasting life.

Jesus did not despise nor did He abhor the affliction of the afflicted but suffered on their behalf. Generally, in taking human likeness and having suffered for the sake of sinners, He identified Himself as the brother of those who believed in Him (cf. Psalms 22:22, 24). Jesus, in particular, of having born as Jew, He said He will treat one, who treats Jews well, as His brother.

"I will declare thy name unto my brethren: in the midst of the congregation will I praise thee" (Psalms 22:22)

"And the King shall answer and say unto them, Verily I say unto you, Inasmuch as ye have done it unto one of the least of these my brethren, ye have done it unto me" (Matthew 25:40)

Man was never in a position to approach God in his fallen nature, and yet God sent His one and only begotten Son for the sake of reconciling us with the Father. We, in the New Testament period, are much more blessed to have access to God so freely than those of Old Testament period. Being conformed to His image, when the Lord comes again, we live and exist in Him.

Jesus became a man of sorrows for our sake and died outside the city and, therefore, He is not ashamed to call those who believe in Him as His brothers. Little before His crucifixion Jesus prayed to the Father that His disciples may be sanctified through His truth.

As for disciples of Jesus or another human sanctification means purification and setting apart for God's work. However, as for Jesus, it was only setting apart for the Father's business and setting free from sin those who believe in Him.

Lord Jesus knew no sin, and He was without any blemish. When He was tried before Governor Pilate, He was not found guilty of death. He was sinless and knew no sin, and He was made sin for our sake in order to redeem us from sin.

"For he hath made him to be sin for us, who knew no sin; that we might be made the righteousness of God in him" (2 Corinthians 5:21)

Jesus Christ, who was the Son of God, says in His prayer to the Father that just as He was set apart and sent into this world, He was sending His disciples into the world. And for their sakes He set apart Himself in order that they may also be sanctified through the truth.

Jesus was not saying in His prayer that His disciples should be moved out from this world to safe havens, but He prayed that they may be kept safe from the evil. He testified that even as the Lord was not of this world, they were also not of the world.

"Sanctify them through thy truth: thy word is truth. As thou hast sent me into the world, even so have I also sent them into the world. And for their sakes I sanctify myself, that they also might be sanctified through the truth". (John 17:17-19)

"And such were some of you: but ye are washed, but ye are sanctified, but ye are justified in the name of the Lord Jesus, and by the Spirit of our God". (1 Corinthians 6:11)

"I pray not that thou shouldest take them out of the world, but that thou shouldest keep them from the evil. They are not of the world, even as I am not of the world". (John 17:15-16)

CHAPTER 5
CROWNED WITH GLORY AND HONOR

"Thou hast put all things in subjection under his feet. For in that he put all in subjection under him, he left nothing that is not put under him. But now we see not yet all things put under him. But we see Jesus, who was made a little lower than the angels for the suffering of death, crowned with glory and honour; that he by the grace of God should taste death for every man" (Hebrews 2:8-9)

In the cool of the day God walked in the Garden of Eden and called Adam and asked him where he was. Adam along with his wife, who was hiding from God, said to the LORD that he was afraid because he was naked (Gen. 3:1-10)

The nakedness in man was not new to God, who created him naked, but the realization that man was naked was that which perplexed man. It was because of man's transgression of God's command that he found himself naked and felt ashamed.

Adam and Eve were deceived by the serpent, and consequently they lost fellowship with God. The LORD said to the serpent that it is cursed above all cattle, and on its belly it shall crawl and eat dust all its life. He continued saying that He will put enmity between its seed, and the seed of the woman, whose seed shall crush its head, and it shall bruise his heel.

Many years later, Lord Jesus, who was the seed of the woman born of Virgin Mary defeated the devil on the cross bearing upon himself, our sin and shame.

Our sin was judged upon the cross. He, who was made little lower than angels, in order that He may die on behalf of us, was crowned with glory and honor.

The LORD said to the woman that He will greatly multiply her sorrow and her conception; and she shall bring forth her children in sorrow, and her desire shall be to her husband who will rule over her; and to Adam the LORD said, the ground shall bring forth thorns and thistles and he shall toil and in sweat he shall eat bread. He continued saying to him that dust that he is made of, unto dust he shall return.

The devil, which is serpent is constantly trying to upset the plans of God by tempting man to yield to his evil plans, and eventually end up in hell, while the LORD took upon Himself the task of redeeming the man from being cast into the 'lake of fire'.

God loved us His only Son Jesus died, and rose from the dead that we may, by believing in Him, enjoy the fellowship with Him, and be conformed to Christ's image. The first redemption was seen when the LORD made coats of skins and clothed Adam and Eve (cf. Genesis 3:1-24), and our redemption is seen in the crucifixion of Jesus as written in Luke 23:1-56 and in other Gospels, as well.

The world would have ended then and there, if God thought of putting an end to Adam and Eve for transgressing His word, but the LORD in His compassion commenced the execution of His plan of salvation from then on. God had put all in subjection under man, and blessed him to have dominion over all creation; but man lost that blessing.

Jesus, the Son of man, who was the only one, who humbled Himself and took a position to be lower than that of angels, has gained the authority over all and crowned with glory.

"Wherefore God also hath highly exalted him, and given him a name which is above every name" (Philippians 2:9)

Lord Jesus Christ, who was equal with the Father, relinquished His glory and came down to this earth to save mankind from being lost eternally. Just before His crucifixion the Lord prayed to the Father to glorify Him because He obeyed the Father and glorified Him.

"These words spake Jesus, and lifted up his eyes to heaven, and said, Father, the hour is come; glorify thy Son, that thy Son also may glorify thee" (John 17:1)

It pleased the Father to bruise His only Son for our sake on the cross that by believing in Him we may have everlasting life. The body of Jesus buried in the tomb did not see corruption and He was raised by the Father on the third day. Jesus was seen by many for forty days on this earth after His resurrection, and was taken up in clouds.

"And when he had spoken these things, while they beheld, he was taken up; and a cloud received him out of their sight" (Acts 1:9)

He will come back in the same way as He was taken up and receive us. As of now, Lord Jesus Christ is seated on the right hand of the Majesty, after purging of our sins, crowned with glory and honor. He took a positon lower than angels for short period of time, in order that He may die on our behalf.

He by the grace of God tasted death on behalf of every man that man by believing in Him should not taste death, which in biblical sense is the spiritual death. The body that is created with the dust has to return to dust, and believer will rise with a glorified body housing his inner man, which is his redeemed soul to be in the Lord.

CHAPTER 6
DECLARATION OF HIS NAME

"Saying, I will declare thy name unto my brethren, in the midst of the church will I sing praise unto thee. And again, I will put my trust in him. And again, Behold I and the children which God hath given me" (Hebrews 2:12-13)

The points for meditation in these two verses are:

- Declaration of His name unto His brethren
- Sing Praises in the midst of the church
- Put trust in Him
- About the children God gave Him

The quote is taken from Psalm Chapter 22 which is Messianic, and in it can be seen some points that that are not applicable to David are surely applicable to Messiah. David was a type of Jesus and his prophetical sayings are shadows of the things to come.

While David declared the name of Jehovah among his brethren, Jesus declared the Father's name among all those who came to Him and called them as His brethren. Nevertheless, Jesus having been a Jewish descendant He also had highest regard for His own brethren, who were Jews.

Referring to His Jewish brethren the Lord said He will treat anyone who helped Jews as His brothers and consider as helping Him.

"And the King shall answer and say unto them, Verily I say unto you, Inasmuch as ye have done it unto one of the least of these my brethren, ye have done it unto me" (Matthew 25:40)

The prophetical sayings of David were literally fulfilled in Jesus, the Messiah. Prophetical sayings of Psalm 22 were literally fulfilled in the life of Jesus when our sin on Him was being judged on the cross. (cf. Psalm 22:1, Matthew 27:46, Psalm 22:8, Matthew 27:43, Psalm 22:18, Matthew 27:35)

This was literally fulfilled which Jesus was on the cross suffering for one and all and our sin was being judged upon the cross. Compare…

"My God, my God, why hast thou forsaken me? why art thou so far from helping me, and from the words of my roaring?" (Psalms 22:1) with

"And about the ninth hour Jesus cried with a loud voice, saying, Eli, Eli, lama sabachthani? that is to say, My God, my God, why hast thou forsaken me?" (Matthew 27:46)

While enemies of David mocked him saying let the LORD, whom he trusted come and deliver him the language used by enemies of Jesus used when He was on the cross, was similar. Compare

"He trusted on the LORD that he would deliver him: let him deliver him, seeing he delighted in him" (Psalms 22:8) with

"He trusted in God; let him deliver him now, if he will have him: for he said, I am the Son of God" (Matthew 27:43)

Compare…

"They part my garments among them, and cast lots upon my vesture". (Psalms 22:18) with

"And they crucified him, and parted his garments, casting lots: that it might be fulfilled which was spoken by the prophet, They parted my garments among them, and upon my vesture did they cast lots" (Matthew 27:35)

The literal fulfillment, in the New Testament, of prophetical sayings of Jesus said thousands of years ago not only in Psalms but in various Old Testament writings show trustworthiness of the scriptures.

Psalmist says He will sing in the midst of the congregation will He praise Him. The Psalm is fully about Jesus who was to come and much of what is not applicable to David in this Psalm was applicable to Messiah; hence this psalm was prophetical and the writer of Hebrews aptly mentions it in application to Jesus the Savior.

Jesus manifested the name and the glory of the Father to His disciples, who in due course of time declared as many as believed in the Lord.

Jesus bore our sin and suffered on the cross on behalf of us, and that is why He was not ashamed to call Himself as the brother of those who believed in Him. Jesus proclaimed the name of the Father among those who believed in Him and He glorified the Father's name.

"I have manifested thy name unto the men which thou gavest me out of the world: thine they were, and thou gavest them me; and they have kept thy word" (John 17:6)

And I have declared unto them thy name, and will declare it: that the love wherewith thou hast loved me may be in them, and I in them. (John 17:26)

In Psalm 22:22 and 23 as Psalmist said that He will declare the name of Jehovah in the midst of the congregation, Jesus the Son of God declared in the midst of the Church the Father's name. He said whoever has seen Him has seen the Father. He and the Father are one, He said.

"I will declare thy name unto my brethren: in the midst of the congregation will I praise thee" (Psalms 22:22)

"Ye that fear the LORD, praise him; all ye the seed of Jacob, glorify him; and fear him, all ye the seed of Israel" (Psalms 22:23)

Not that Jesus disregarded His mother when He asked question as to who is mother was, and who His brothers were, but His purpose of asking that question was to reveal the truth that He being God Himself, whoever heard the word of God and did it were His mothers and brothers (cf. Matt 28:10, Luke 8:21).

After the resurrection of Jesus when Mary tried to touch Him he said to her to go to His brothers and say to them that He would ascend soon to His Father.

"Jesus saith unto her, Touch me not; for I am not yet ascended to my Father: but go to my brethren, and say unto them, I ascend unto my Father, and your Father; and to my God, and your God" (John 20:17)

CHAPTER 7
MEDIATOR OF BETTER COVENANT

But now hath he obtained a more excellent ministry, by how much also he is the mediator of a better covenant, which was established upon better promises. (Hebrews 8:6)

The New covenant was the best of all the covenants that we could receive. The Old covenants included in them the shadows of new things to come, which paved the way for the Old Testament saints also to be saved under the grace just as we are saved.

Old Testament law was stringent in nature, which demanded unconditional obedience without sinning, whereas the New Testament covenant included in it obedience sincerely, which is done through the grace.

But seek ye first the kingdom of God, and his righteousness; and all these things shall be added unto you. (Matthew 6:33)

Repentance of sins to Jesus and accepting him as Lord and believing that God raised Him from the dead on the third day is sufficient to be saved and that is achieved through the grace bestowed upon us by Lord Jesus Christ, who is the only mediator between man and the Father in heaven.

Jesus said, in John 5:43 "I am come in my Father's name, and ye receive me not: if another shall come in his own name, him ye will receive", and in John 14:13 "And whatsoever ye shall ask in my name, that will I do, that the Father may be glorified in the Son". Jesus also said, in John 10:30 "I and my Father are one".

The way the sins are forgiven of those in Old Testament period differs a great deal from the way the sins are forgiven of the ones in the New Testament period.

In the Old Testament period only the high priest could enter the "Holy of Holies" and only once. Their sins were covered by not wholly forgiven until Jesus died a substitutionary death on the cross. He died for our sins, was buried and was raised from the dead by God and then after appearing to many He ascended into heaven and is seated at the right hand of the Majesty.

Although, Aaron was priest, yet he and his children had to purify themselves first, before they could minister to others (Exodus 29:1) whereas Jesus was sinless and without any blemish.

Forasmuch as ye know that ye were not redeemed with corruptible things, as silver and gold, from your vain conversation received by tradition from your fathers; But with the precious blood of Christ, as of a lamb without blemish and without spot: (1 Peter 1:18-19)

The righteousness is imputed on all, who believe in Jesus and it is free through grace.

Even the righteousness of God which is by faith of Jesus Christ unto all and upon all them that believe: for there is no difference: (Romans 3:22)

Moses was called by God to deliver His people physically from the bondage of slavery under Pharaoh. Even though his first reaction was to reject the call of God, he finally yielded and obeyed the LORD's . Moses was known for his genuine and reasonable anger certain times, common to any man, firstly in breaking the first set of tablets containing Ten Commandments, secondly in arguing with God on behalf of Israelites, who rebelled against God, and thirdly in deviation from the instructions from God by striking the rock when he was supposed to speak to the rock to fetch the water for Israelites. Yet, Moses was considered as the meekest of all men.

(Now the man Moses was very meek, above all the men which were upon the face of the earth.) (Numbers 12:3)

Similar type of genuine and reasonable anger was seen in the Son of Man, Jesus, when the temple, where the Father in heaven was to be honored, was used by merchants, to sell their merchandise.

If we read Matthew 21:12 we find that, "... Jesus went into the temple of God, and cast out all them that sold and bought in the temple, and overthrew the tables of the moneychangers, and the seats of them that sold doves". God takes it very serious if his temple is desecrated and dishonored with worldly things. Here Jesus saw that the temple, which was a worship place, was used for a wrong purpose.

Jews, however, did not consider it profane to allow merchandise in the premise of the temple inasmuch as it was easy for them to buy things used for worship and sacrifice, yet on the whole the trade and transactions gave rise to great deal of noise, confusion and disturbance to the true worshippers.

This place was also used by money exchangers to convert Jewish coins in to Roman coins which gave rise to much noise and confusion. This place was also used for selling doves, which are, of course, used as sacrifice elements during worship, yet the scene produced a great deal of noise and confusion.

The crux of the problem here was the merchants misused the porch and the temple area for selling their merchandise thinking that those who need them for worship may use them and the place would be an easy access to them, yet the problem that such merchandise and the transactions within and without the temple area disturbed the worship service, and caused great deal of confusion within the temple.

Jesus was greater than Moses in all aspects and His blood, which was without any blemish, was all sufficient to cleanse us from all our sins provided we accept Him as Lord and we repent of our sins and by believing that God raised Him from the dead on the third day.

That if thou shalt confess with thy mouth the Lord Jesus, and shalt believe in thine heart that God hath raised him from the dead, thou shalt be saved. For with the heart man believeth unto righteousness; and with the mouth confession is made unto salvation. (Romans 10:9-10)

Repent ye therefore, and be converted, that your sins may be blotted out, when the times of refreshing shall come from the presence of the Lord; (Acts 3:19)

CHAPTER 8
JESUS IS GREATER THAN MOSES

"And Moses verily was faithful in all his house, as a servant, for a testimony of those things which were to be spoken after; But Christ as a son over his own house; whose house are we, if we hold fast the confidence and the rejoicing of the hope firm unto the end" (Hebrews 3:5-6)

If not for the misunderstanding that Moses is the savior, why would Israel still consider him above Lord Jesus Christ? No doubt the children of Israel are chosen ones above all other nations and God blessed them. It should be our desire that God may continue to bless them to have their position before the LORD just as the LORD desired them to have. Pray for the peace of Jerusalem.

It is because of their repeated rebellions against God that there is a postponement of full care for them in the present situation. God has undying love for them and no one should hate them because in the very early chapters of the Pentateuch God said whoever curses Abraham, him will the LORD curse, and whoever blesses Abraham, him will the LORD bless.

"And I will bless them that bless thee, and curse him that curseth thee: and in thee shall all families of the earth be blessed" (Genesis 12:3)

The second part of the blessing reads "in thee shall all families of the earth be blessed". Israel is the blessed name given for Abraham's grandson Jacob. Moses was the leader of the children of Israel, who were redeemed from the bondage of slavery under Pharaoh. Moses led the children of Israel as a faithful servant of the LORD from Egypt unto Canaan, but not into Canaan.

The reason why all those who left Egypt perished in the wilderness was because they all rebelled against the LORD; and this includes their leader Moses, who struck the rock twice to get the water out of it, in disobedience to the LORD's command that he should speak to the rock and get the water out of it. God did not allow Moses to enter into the Promised Land; however, he was given privilege to see it from far distance. Moses could not lead the children of Israel into God's rest (cf. Psalm 95:11, Heb. 13-17-18).

New Testament has strong supporting words for Gentiles that whosoever believes in Lord Jesus Christ and asserts faith in Him, will be saved from eternal damnation.

Abraham believed in God and it was counted to Him as righteousness. Although Gentiles are not his posterity, yet they receive the same blessings as do the children of Israel by exercising faith in Jesus. This was the good news given to Abraham that in him shall all the nations and every tongue confessing Jesus as Lord will be blessed.

"Even as Abraham believed God, and it was accounted to him for righteousness. Know ye therefore that they which are of faith, the same are the children of Abraham. And the scripture, foreseeing that God would justify the heathen through faith, preached before the gospel unto Abraham, saying, In thee shall all nations be blessed. So then they which be of faith are blessed with faithful Abraham" (Galatians 3:6-9)

"For we which have believed do enter into rest, as he said, As I have sworn in my wrath, if they shall enter into my rest:

although the works were finished from the foundation of the world" (Hebrews 4:3)

Joshua the son of Nun and Caleb the son of Jephunneh, who did not drift from the faith in the LORD and the children of Israel born in the wilderness were the only ones who could enter the Promised Land. Joshua circumcised, in the Promised Land, all those who could not be circumcised in the wilderness.

As the history of Israel shows us, the children of Israel, who have entered into the Promised Land also rebelled against the LORD and reaped the consequences. Thus, even though God blessed them abundantly they temporarily lost their blessings and eventually they are made blind to the truth that Jesus is the Messiah.

Inasmuch as there is no temple for them, and they are not sacrificing animals now, they have no method for forgiveness of their sins now, unless they believe in Jesus Christ.

Lord Jesus came in flesh in the likeness of man to redeem mankind from sin that whoever believes in Him shall not perish but have everlasting life. His incarnation was according to several promises in the Old Testament.

The children of Israel are still waiting for Messiah to come with the belief that their Messiah will come like a man, who would make the world perfect. They believe that no man on earth until now has fulfilled qualifications to be their Messiah.

The children of Israel have not yet taken into consideration that Jesus was their Messiah and because of their unbelief in Him many prophecies that were to be fulfilled in His life time, were postponed to future. All the prophecies prophesied about the future will surely be fulfilled. Lord Jesus Christ was born in human likeness into the lineage of David, and will come as the 'Lion of the tribe of Judah' and will rule the nations from the throne of David for a thousand years, and will continue thereafter after fully defeating Satan.

The promises contained in Isaiah 2:4 that He 'will judge nations', Isaiah 26:19 that 'dead men shall live', Daniel 12:2 that those who are 'sleeping in the dust of earth shall awake', Jeremiah 23:5-6 that David's descendant will be a king, who 'shall reign and prosper', Ezekiel 37:26-28 that His 'tabernacle shall be with them', Zechariah 14:9 that 'the LORD shall be king over all the earth' belong to future.

One should have faith that those prophecies will be fulfilled. It seems like they want God to tread their path of beliefs, as quickly as possible, rather than wait for God to fulfill the promises according to His plan and purpose.

God has definite purpose of saving Gentiles as well. There is a time and plan laid out by God to bring Nations to salvation; and when the fulness of the said time is come, Jesus will return and fulfill all promises about future.

Moses was faithful servant in the LORD's house "for a testimony of those things which were to be spoken after." However, Lord Jesus Christ, who is the Son of God, was and is surely greater than Moses inasmuch as He was faithful in His own house that He built. He is the builder and we are His living stones.

CHAPTER 9
FAITHFUL HIGH PRIEST

"Wherefore in all things it behoved him to be made like unto his brethren, that he might be a merciful and faithful high priest in things pertaining to God, to make reconciliation for the sins of the people. For in that he himself hath suffered being tempted, he is able to succor them that are tempted" (Hebrews 2:17-18)

Inspired by the Holy Spirit the writer of the Book of Hebrews enlisted the great attributes of Lord Jesus Christ in the first two chapters starting with the description of God, who spoke to men in different periods in different ways and in the last days by Lord Jesus Christ, the Son of God, who is the exact imprint of the Father, and after the Lord had purged our sins sat down on the right hand of the Majesty on high.

Secondly, the superiority of Jesus, who even though He was superior to angels, had ethical consideration to humble Himself to become a man, a position lesser than the angels to qualify Himself to be offered as sacrifice for the sake of man's salvation.

Thereafter, we read a short note in Hebrews 2:17-18, how Jesus becomes faithful high priest to plead with the Father on behalf of us, the details of which follow in subsequent chapters.

It is quite known to all Christians how Satan rebelled against God by setting in his proud heart the thoughts of becoming like God and eventually was thrown out from the presence of God. Satan left along with the group of fallen angels the Lord's presence and formed another kingdom of which Jesus referred to in Matthew 12:26.

"And if Satan cast out Satan, he is divided against himself; how shall then his kingdom stand?" (Matthew 12:26)

Even though Satan left the presence of God he had access to heaven as we read in Job 1st Chapter. It was God who challenged Satan if he saw that Job was righteous. Satan said to God that Job's obedience and righteousness are the result of the LORD laying hedge around Job, and if that hedge was removed Job would curse God.

The LORD gave permission to Satan to lay hands on Job, except that he cannot touch Job's life. Job endured all the tests and comes out the test successfully to prove that he was indeed righteous.

There are two points here. God protected Job's soul from destruction. Satan had access to the throne even after his falling from the presence of God. The final destruction of Satan is prophesied as being in Armageddon war, which is yet to happen. This gives a clear understanding to us that there is no salvation for Satan.

As for man's rebellion, if God did not show His love and mercy toward mankind all of us would have also perished in 'lake of fire' just as Satan would be cast finally into it.

In order that man may not be lost forever, because God created man in His own image, God sent His only Son Jesus into this world taking the likeness, nothing greater than man, or nothing less than man but in the likeness of man.

Jesus did not take the likeness of angels because He was not denoted to the office of saving angels. He did not take any likeness below in dignity than that of man because He was appointed to the office of saving mankind from damnation.

The Book of Acts shows us that God is Triune: the Father, the Son, and the Holy Spirit. God came down into this world in the person of Jesus in the likeness of man.

"Until the day in which he was taken up, after that he through the Holy Ghost had given commandments unto the apostles whom he had chosen" (Acts 1:2)

"Ye men of Israel, hear these words; Jesus of Nazareth, a man approved of God among you by miracles and wonders and signs, which God did by him in the midst of you, as ye yourselves also know" (Acts 2:22)

If God died then there would have been no God causing anarchy and let such a thought be abhorred, but God in the likeness of man died for our sake and was raised from death. God is eternal and He lives forever, and His name is above all the names and He may be exalted above everything and everyone.

Lord Jesus took a body of flesh and blood because the children of God whom He was going to save are made of flesh and blood. He took the body of flesh and blood out of His mercy in order to show His love and mercy toward mankind who are of flesh and blood.

By His own sacrifice of His body of flesh and blood He became mediator between God and man and thus became the high priest for us to plead on behalf of us continually and to the cause of perseverance of believers until the end in order to see that our salvation is not lost.

No truly born-again child will willfully reject Jesus as savior or commit sins deliberately in order to be repeatedly saved.

Temptations for man are common and God does not subject us to any temptation greater than that cannot be overcome; rather He always provides way for escaping from the temptations. Jesus Himself was tempted by the devil and He overcame temptations and that is why He is able to provide succor to those who are tempted.

CHAPTER 10
WE ARE HIS WORKMANSHIP

There are two passages that can be considered under this title.

Firstly, the words of Lord Jesus Christ, who says...

"I am the vine, ye are the branches: He that abideth in me, and I in him, the same bringeth forth much fruit: for without me ye can do nothing. If a man abide not in me, he is cast forth as a branch, and is withered; and men gather them, and cast them into the fire, and they are burned. If ye abide in me, and my words abide in you, ye shall ask what ye will, and it shall be done unto you. Herein is my Father glorified, that ye bear much fruit; so shall ye be my disciples" (John 15:5-8)

Lord Jesus was not saying here that the salvation of all those who do not remain in Him as branches receiving sap from the root will be lost, and they will be cast into hellfire; but He says if we do not remain in Him we will be cut off from the power source, and cannot achieve any good results by our works.

The Almighty God is glorified when we bear much fruit and remain as His disciples. Just as Abraham was the root of the 'olive' tree in the Old Testament period, Jesus is the root of the 'vine' in the New Testament period.

The Lord says if we do not remain in Him we will be cut off and we will wither. Men gather the withered branches and cast them into the fire. On the contrary if we remain in Him we will not only bear fruit for Him but our prayers said in accordance with His will and purpose will be answered

Secondly, the words of Apostle Paul, who says...

"For we are his workmanship, created in Christ Jesus unto good works, which God hath before ordained that we should walk in them" (Ephesians 2:10)

Our good works do not precede our salvation but they follow us. It is by faith in Lord Jesus Christ that we are saved. It confirms that good works that we do before receiving salvation, although they are good service in human sense keeping good conscience, yet they will not be the cause for our salvation.

None of the good works that we do before accepting Jesus as savior will entail us to have place in heaven. After we are saved, God shows us our role in doing well for others. We are foreordained to do good works by God because we are His workmanship and we glorify not only Him but also His works.

"Christ is become of no effect unto you, whosoever of you are justified by the law; ye are fallen from grace" (Galatians 5:4 KJV)

"You who are trying to be justified by the law have been alienated from Christ; you have fallen away from grace" (Galatians 5:4 NIV)

Greek word "ekpipto" (Strong's number 1601), means "to drop away; specially, be driven out of one's course; figuratively, to lose, become inefficient" and this is the word translated as "fallen from" in Galatians 5:4, which is to say that whoever is justified by the Mosaic Law is out from the purview of "Grace".

The Law points to sin and never to the salvation; and by keeping Mosaic Law no one is justified nor will ever be justified righteous, and the Scripture says...

"As it is written, There is none righteous, no, not one" (Romans 3:10)

And Jesus said...

"I came not to call the righteous, but sinners to repentance" (Luke 5:32)

Apostle Paul corroborates the instructions Jesus gave and says whoever tries to be justified by the Mosaic Law ignoring that which the Lord has done for us, is fallen from the grace of God.

Fundamentally, it is by grace through faith that we are saved and not by our own good works, lest anyone should boast that one received salvation by his own efforts. We wait through the Spirit for the hope of righteousness by faith.

Neither circumcision nor any of our good works or uncircumcision or any legalistic belief, or trying to find a deity on a hill by climbing several thousand steps will give us salvation. It is only faith in Lord Jesus Christ and the efficacy of His blood shed on the cross on our behalf will bring us salvation.

It is imperative that we do not lose our soul (inner-self) to eternal damnation. Bible says faith in Jesus enables us to love one another and therefore, Paul questions if all these be true then why should a believer, who ran his race well in keeping the faith should fall back or drop away from one's course in Jesus. The Lord helps us not fall into the temptations of this world. He helps us to serve Him and to bring forth fruit unto Him. .

CHAPTER 11
AUTHORITY NOT TO THE ANGELS

"For unto the angels hath he not put in subjection the world to come, whereof we speak" (Hebrews 2:5)

The world to come is not subject to the angels but to the one who is superior to angels, and He is Lord Jesus Christ. It was that world in the Old Testament period, where angels had to do the disposition of the Law, and mediate between men and God. Angels visited Abram (cf. Genesis 18:2). They helped the children of Israel in their battles. When the phrase is written as "the angel of the LORD" it fundamentally meant pre-incarnate Jesus.

"And it came to pass that night, that the angel of the LORD went out, and smote in the camp of the Assyrians an hundred fourscore and five thousand: and when they arose early in the morning, behold, they were all dead corpses" (2 Kings 19:35)

A mighty angel Michael fought with the devil for the body of Moses, and said to the devil "let the Lord rebuke thee".

"Yet Michael the archangel, when contending with the devil he disputed about the body of Moses, durst not bring against him a railing accusation, but said, The Lord rebuke thee" (Jude 1:9)

Some teach an error that Jesus was Michael the angel but the description in Jude 1:9 and 1 Thessalonians 4:16-17 show that Jesus was not the Michael the Archangel. Jesus was eternally with God, and He was the begotten Son of God, and as the Lord proclaimed He and the Father are one.

"In the beginning was the Word, and the Word was with God, and the Word was God" (John 1:1)

A messenger from God said to Daniel, "....Fear not, Daniel: for from the first day that thou didst set thine heart to understand, and to chasten thyself before thy God, thy words were heard, and I am come for thy words" (Daniel 10:12)

It was Michael, the archangel, who fought with the angel of darkness, the representation of the Persian world power, which prevented the messenger for twenty one days from God visiting Daniel (Twenty one days are a period of time when Daniel was mourning for three weeks).

"But the prince of the kingdom of Persia withstood me one and twenty days: but, lo, Michael, one of the chief princes, came to help me; and I remained there with the kings of Persia" (Daniel 10:13)

For a certain period of time in the New Testament period until Jesus was born angels mediated between God and men. Angel Gabriel gave glad tidings to Zechariah that Elizabeth his wife will have a son, and because he did not believe he was made dumb until John, the Baptist was born to them. (cf. Luke 1:19, 22).

Angel Gabriel visited Joseph and said to take Mary as His wife, even though she was pregnant because the baby in her womb was Holy one, the result of the overshadowing of Holy Spirit on her (cf. Luke 1:26). The angel of the Lord visited shepherds and gave them the good news of the birth of Lord Jesus (cf. Luke 2:9-11)

However, Lord Jesus being superior to angels and obedient even to the point of death on the wretched cross, and offered

Himself as sacrifice, once for all on behalf of us, to redeem us from the bondage of sin and hellfire, the Father gave all the authority to Him.

The world to come was future, when Jesus and Paul were on this earth, and it meant primarily the age we live in i.e. the Church Age, and it secondarily meant the millennial kingdom, and thereafter.

Although Church came into existence on the fiftieth day after the resurrection of Jesus, it came into present form much later as One New Man with Jews and Gentiles one in Him. (Ephesians 3:3-6). Lord Jesus Christ is the head of the church.

After the second advent of Jesus, He will the rule the earth from the throne of David, and will continue to have His authority over all, whether it be in heaven, or in earth. He will judge the quick and the dead. Whoever confesses Him as Lord and believes in heart that God raised Him from the dead on the third day will have everlasting life.

The LORD, therefore, did not subject the world to come to angels. Those who are born again will rise from the dead, and those who are alive, when He comes, will be caught up to Him to be with Him forever and ever. This is the first resurrection. All those who are not saved will rise at the end of the age to be judged at the Great White Throne to be cast into the burning 'lake of fire' along with death and hell, and Satan.

CHAPTER 12
TO DESTROY THE DEVIL

"Forasmuch then as the children are partakers of flesh and blood, he also himself likewise took part of the same; that through death he might destroy him that had the power of death, that is, the devil" (Hebrews 2:14)

There are four points to ponder in Hebrews 2:14 and they are...

- Children are partakers of flesh and blood
- Jesus took part of flesh and blood
- Devil had the power over death
- Jesus by His death destroyed the Devil

All those who believed in Jesus are the children of God and interestingly the children's children are not grandchildren of God, but they are also children. The privilege given to the children of God is that as many as received Him and believed on His name (not selected lot; but as many as received Him) are given the privilege of becoming the sons of God (cf. John 1:12, Romans 10:9)

We have not received the spirit of bondage, but the spirit of adoption and that is the reason why we are able to call God as our Abba, Father (cf. Romans 8:15, Galatians 4:6)

We are adopted sons and daughters and on our resurrection we attain glorified bodies such as that of the resurrected body of Lord Jesus Christ. The Lord is our portion and we inherit our blessings in Him. We will be conformed to His image.

Our bodies are made of flesh and blood and by birth we are sinners, according to Romans 5:12 and therefore, death had power over us but Satan has no right to take the life of Jesus, who was sinless. Man lost not only authority over creation, but also lost earth and eternal life by transgressing God's command.

Jesus humbled Himself to become flesh and blood for our sake, born of the Virgin Mary, and lived a holy life consecrated unto God for the specific purpose of redeeming mankind from the bondage of sin. He took upon Himself our sin and died on the cross to defeat the devil.

In order to redeem us from the fleshly body which houses our soul, Jesus took the likeness of man and lived in this world as a man and died for us in flesh and blood. He took part of the flesh and blood in order that all the children of God may receive glorified bodies and receive everlasting life (cf. John 1:14).

"For as in Adam all die, even so in Christ shall all be made alive" (1 Corinthians 15:22)

"In a moment, in the twinkling of an eye, at the last trump: for the trumpet shall sound, and the dead shall be raised incorruptible, and we shall be changed" (1 Corinthians 15:52)

The Lord's purpose of coming into this world was not only to save us from sin, but also to destroy the devil which had the power to cause the death. The death was introduced in man's life by the devil and he gained the power to cause death in man because man sinned and lost fellowship with God.

The devil had no power of Lord Jesus Christ, because the Lord is the Son of God. He did not sin anyway and was holy and without any blemish. He was just and did not deserve death penalty, and yet the devil made every attempt to murder the

Son of God. It was unlawful, and the devil was responsible for causing unlawful death to Jesus.

Lord Jesus said He has the power to lay down His life and take it back again and as such no one could take His life. It pleased the Father to bruise His one and only Son for our sake in order that by accepting Him as Lord any sinner could be saved and receive everlasting life.

By allowing Satan to resort to unlawful killing of Jesus, God fulfilled His purpose, and thus the prophecy that the seed of the woman shall bruise the devil's head is fulfilled. It was the first prophecy in the Bible.

"And I will put enmity between thee and the woman, and between thy seed and her seed; it shall bruise thy head, and thou shalt bruise his heel" (Genesis 3:15)

This is the purpose that God had planned to achieve and He achieved it. Satan bruised His heel but the Lord bruised Satan's head and defeated him.

CHAPTER 13
PARTAKERS OF HEAVENLY CALLING

"Wherefore, holy brethren, partakers of the heavenly calling, consider the Apostle and High Priest of our profession, Christ Jesus; Who was faithful to him that appointed him, as also Moses was faithful in all his house. For this man was counted worthy of more glory than Moses, inasmuch as he who hath builded the house hath more honour than the house. For every house is builded by some man; but he that built all things is God" (Hebrews 3:1-4)

In the preceding two chapters it was established that Jesus, who is exact image of the invisible God the Father, is the Son of God, and that He is superior to angels, yet He took a position lower than that of angels for the sake of reconciling man with God. In the last two verses of Hebrews Chapter 2 a glimpse of the greatness of the Lord Jesus Christ, who is faithful High priest, is shown.

Here, in these verses there is admonition for all the believers, whom God called as brethren of Lord Jesus Christ, to take note of the heavenly blessings they are bestowed with, and of being made partakers of the heavenly calling.

There is also warning to understand that Jesus is superior to angels and Moses, and therefore, not to rebel against Him, lest they should face rigorous chastisement than those children of Israel, who left Egypt for Canaan, could not make it to the Promised Land, but perished in the wilderness. Let everyone acknowledge that inasmuch as God is the builder of the house, wherein Moses was a faithful servant, and Lord Jesus, who was the Son of God, is worthy of more glory and greater than Moses.

While God chose Israel as a nation and as His people, and Moses as their leader, Lord Jesus is the head of the Church, and He is in the midst of the Church. The Scripture gives description of Jesus.

"And he is the head of the body, the church: who is the beginning, the firstborn from the dead; that in all things he might have the preeminence. For it pleased the Father that in him should all fulness dwell; And, having made peace through the blood of his cross, by him to reconcile all things unto himself; by him, I say, whether they be things in earth, or things in heaven" (Colossians 1:18-20)

Hebrews Chapter 3 begins with word "wherefore" indicating the importance of the previous narration in chapters that believers, who had heavenly calling and having responded to that call, are blessed and became the Lord's brothers.

An interesting point next is to consider whether Jesus was an angel, or apostle or high priest. The book of Revelation shows that Jesus was the only one worthy to open the seven seals of the scroll. Angels had different roles, and Jesus was never presented as an angel.

In Chapters 1 and 2 of Hebrews, it was established undoubtedly that Jesus was not an angel, but He was greater than angels. He did not take the likeness of an angel, or lived as a Spirit being; neither did He take the likeness of anyone below in dignity than that of a man. He took the likeness of man, in order to qualify Himself to purge man's sins. He said on the cross "It is finished", indicating that He finished the work assigned to Him by the Father, and thereafter ascended into heaven to sit on the right hand of the Majesty in high. It pleased the Father to bruise Him for our sake.

Seldom do we call Jesus as an apostle for the simple reason that it creates confusion and controversy in discussions. Nonetheless, in the light of few references it is not wrong to identify Jesus by the title "apostle".

"And they answered Jesus, and said, We cannot tell. And he said unto them, Neither tell I you by what authority I do these things" (Matthew 21:27)

"Then said Jesus to them again, Peace be unto you: as my Father hath sent me, even so send I you" (John 20:21)

Hebrews 3:1 is the only place in the Bible, where Jesus is called as an apostle. The word 'apostle' means 'sent'. He was sent into this world as an Ambassador from heaven. God sent His one and only Son Jesus into this world that whoever believes in Him shall not perish but have everlasting life.

Inasmuch as Lord Jesus Christ gave us a better covenant than that was in Old Testament, and also by offering His own body as sacrifice, rather than offering animals as sacrifice by the Old Testament high priest, Jesus is our High Priest.

After the fall of man he could not approach God just as he had fellowship with God in the cool of the day in the Garden of Eden. God chose priests from the tribe of Levi, and it was from among them that the mediator Moses became the leader. Subsequently Aaronic order of priesthood was established.

While daily sacrifices were offered by priests, the sacrifice for the nation of Israel could be done only by Aaron the high priest, or his descendants, who alone could enter the Holy of Holies in the Tabernacle and sprinkle the blood of Lord's goat on the mercy seat, and thereafter confess sins of the people on the scapegoat outside the Tabernacle, and from where the scapegoat was sent away to wilderness never to return again.

Greater sacrifice was made by Lord Jesus Christ. He offered His own flesh and body on the cross for our sake, and that is how He became our High Priest of the order of Melchizedek rendering easy access for every believer to approach God.

When the curtain in the Temple was rent from top to bottom by the power of the Almighty God, the privilege of worshipping and praying to the Almighty God straight in the name of Jesus Christ was given to everyone, whether of Jew or of Gentile.

Jesus is our mediator and there is, therefore, no other priest is required to be in the middle between God and men. Thus Lord Jesus Christ has become superior to Moses.

"And as they were eating, Jesus took bread, and blessed it, and brake it, and gave it to the disciples, and said, Take, eat; this is my body" (Matthew 26:26)

"I am the vine, ye are the branches: He that abideth in me, and I in him, the same bringeth forth much fruit: for without me ye can do nothing." (John 15:5)

"I am crucified with Christ: nevertheless I live; yet not I, but Christ liveth in me: and the life which I now live in the flesh I live by the faith of the Son of God, who loved me, and gave himself for me" (Galatians 2:20)

CHAPTER 14
OUR RIGHTS IN THE LORD

"But as many as received him, to them gave he power to become the sons of God, even to them that believe on his name: Which were born, not of blood, nor of the will of the flesh, nor of the will of man, but of God" (John 1:12-13)

As the new year dawns upon us let us meditate from the Scriptures the rights and privileges we are given to enjoy in the Lord. Just as we were driving the other day it came to my mind what if people did not know their rights and privileges on the road.

Indeed, it is hard for people in certain countries to understand or follow the concept of 'right-of-way' while driving.

Where there is no such 'right-of-way' law or where there is violation of such law, the consequences are catastrophic, immediate and long-lasting.

Is it not worth pondering on our rights and privileges which God gave to us? There is a 'right of way' given for those who believe in Jesus. The believers in Jesus have great rights and privileges. John the Gospel writer describes God, His Word, and the rights and privileges of born-again children. The very first verse of the first chapter of John's Gospel contains unfathomable knowledge.

The verse reads...

"In the beginning was the Word, and the Word was with God, and the Word was God" (John 1:1)

The LORD is Almighty God and He says…

"And who, as I, shall call, and shall declare it, and set it in order for me, since I appointed the ancient people? and the things that are coming, and shall come, let them shew unto them?" (Isaiah 44:7)

Bible does not say that "the Word was a god" but firmly states that "The Word was God". It is not a common article used but a definite one i.e., "the" is used. He was with the God and He was in the beginning. What was the beginning then? Genesis 1:1 reads…

"In the beginning God created the heaven and the earth" (Genesis 1:1)

We have no information as to when that "beginning" was and from what point it should be understood as "the beginning". God is eternal, He existed, He now exists and He will exist. He called His name as "I AM that I AM". He is always in the present tense.

It is clear from John 1:1-2 and Philippians 2:6-7 that Jesus was with the Father partaking of the divine glory. In His incarnation He came down in the form of servant and in the likeness of man relinquishing His glory.

God created light before he created Sun and Moon, which He put them in their respective positions to distinguish the time and seasons, days and years.

"And God said, Let there be light: and there was light. And God saw the light, that it was good: and God divided the light from the darkness" (Genesis 1:3-4)

"And God said, Let there be lights in the firmament of the heaven to divide the day from the night; and let them be for signs, and for seasons, and for days, and years" (Genesis 1:14)

"The true light, which gives light to everyone, was coming into the world. He was in the world, and the world was made through him, yet the world did not know him. He came to his own, and his own people did not receive him. But to all who did receive him, who believed in his name, he gave the right to become children of God, who were born, not of blood nor of the will of the flesh nor of the will of man, but of God" (John 1:9-13)

"And God said, 'Let there be light,' and there was light. And God saw that the light was good. And God separated the light from the darkness. God called the light Day, and the darkness he called Night. And there was evening and there was morning, the first day" (Genesis 1:2-5)

"All things were made by him; and without him was not any thing made that was made. In him was life; and the life was the light of men. And the light shineth in darkness; and the darkness comprehended it not". (John 1:3-5)

Darkness in a room flees immediately when a speck of light flashes into it. Darkness did not comprehend the power of the light.

Darkness tried to be reigning, but when the light came in, the darkness disappeared. When God breathed the breath of life into the nostrils of man, made of dust of the ground, the man became a living soul.

The Father is the source of life, and as the Father has life in Him, so does He gave to the Son to have life in Him, and the Son came down from heaven and gave life into the world. (cf. John 5:26; 33)

Jesus said: "...I am the way, the truth, and the life: no man cometh unto the Father, but by me" (John 14:6)

Those who are unaware of "Trinity" will get confused as to who the Father is, who the Son of God is, and who the Holy Spirit is! There are several references in the Bible that the Father, the Son and the Holy Spirit are One. They are not three Gods but One in Three, co-equal, co-existent.

Jesus said: "I and my Father are one" (John 10:30)

To as many as (not few or select few), but all who believe in Jesus, He gave the power to become the sons of God. What a great privilege is given to those who believe in Lord Jesus Christ! They are given the power to become the sons of God. The children of children are not grandchildren of God but they too are the 'sons of God'.

All those who believe in the Lord will become 'the sons of God'. It certainly does not mean they will become equal with God or Lord Jesus Christ, who alone is the begotten 'Son of God'; nevertheless when the Lord comes all those who are saved by the precious blood of Jesus Christ will be conformed to His image.

It speaks of spiritual relationship and not of human/fleshly relationship. They are not born of blood, or according to the flesh, or of the will of man, but of God. It is the Royal gift conferred on them, and it is absolutely divine.

Lord Jesus Christ is the 'Son of God' and He was not made to be so, but He is eternal. God sent His only Son into this world in order that whoever believes in Him should not perish but have everlasting life.

"For God so loved the world, that he gave his only begotten Son, that whosoever believeth in him should not perish, but have everlasting life". (John 3:16)

The "Word" was made flesh and He lived among us and John and others saw His glory, which was full of grace and truth.

"And the Word was made flesh, and dwelt among us, (and we beheld his glory, the glory as of the only begotten of the Father,) full of grace and truth". (John 1:14)

The Lord was in the world, which was made by Him but the world did not know Him. He came to His own but they rejected Him.

"He was in the world, and the world was made by him, and the world knew him not. He came unto his own, and his own received him not" (John 1:10-11)

Inasmuch as we are the children of light and the children of the day, and not in darkness that that day should overtake us, nor are we children of darkness let us respond, in the New Year, to the Lord, who said "...Surely I come quickly", by saying "...Amen.

Even so, come, Lord Jesus..." (cf. 1 Thessalonians 5:4-5 and Revelation 22:20-21)

CHAPTER 15
LAW OUR SCHOOL MASTER

"Wherefore the law was our schoolmaster to bring us unto Christ, that we might be justified by faith" (Galatians 3:24)

It is the Mosaic Law given by God to the children of Israel, and not the secular law, which Paul talks about here, and therefore, there would be some who may have questions as to why God, initially demanded that His Laws should be followed by them, and then allowed 'grace' to take prominence in the New Testament period.

Apostle Paul writes that the law is not against the promises of God, but it was given in order that man may understand that the transgressions he committed cannot be forgiven by law, which only points out the guilt of a person.

Under the law priest had to offer sacrifice first for himself and then offer a sacrifice for the person, who is guilty. If law could make a person righteous, then truly righteousness should have been by law, but the Scripture has concluded all under sin.

The promise by faith of Lord Jesus Christ was made available only to those who believe. The law was our schoolmaster in order to teach us the way unto Jesus, who is the only mediator. We can be justified only by faith in him.

After Jesus had become propitiation for us, it is not required of us to do what was to be done under the law, in order to receive salvation. Faith in the Lord Jesus Christ alone is enough; and that is to say that we are no longer under schoolmaster.

As many as have believed and accepted Jesus Christ as personal Savior and Lord, have put on Christ, irrespective of whether they are Jew or Greek, bond or free, or male or female.

All those, who are saved by the precious blood of Jesus Christ, are one in Him. We, therefore, belong to Him and are Abraham's seed by faith and thus have inherited the promises.

Apostle Paul blesses those, who accept Christ's death upon the cross and His resurrection, rather than subjecting themselves voluntarily to be under the yoke of Mosaic Law. He says fulfilling the Law of Christ is more important than that of the Old Testament Laws.

No one should boast of himself nor glory himself/herself, but everyone should glorify Lord Jesus Christ, whose marks were borne by not only Apostle Paul but all those, who realize the efficacy of the blood of Lord Jesus Christ.

Paul's feels as if he was under the travail of child birth to explain to Galatians the difference between Law and Grace, and how hard it is to be under the yoke of Law rather than accept salvation by "Grace" alone. He calls them, now, "my little children", and tries to explain to them about the implications in believing that Law and Works only would save them.

Galatians were under the erroneous belief that Law and Works only can save them. They desired to take pride in a list of rules they prescribed for themselves and believe that as they keep set of rules they would become perfect. In other words, it renders a notion that man can earn his salvation by keeping a set of rules, like being good and doing well to others etc. Those things, undoubtedly help men to be called as 'good men' but that would not secure salvation to have everlasting life, which is available, free of cost, only as a result of belief in the finished works of Jesus, the Son of God, who did for men.

Lord Jesus Christ did it all to earn salvation for us. He finished all that we need to do to earn salvation and it is, therefore, mandatory that we should believe in His finished work for our salvation, rather than finding our own ways to get saved.

Jesus came down into this world to redeem us from the bondage of sin, and, therefore, He took upon himself, our transgressions, and died substitutionary death on behalf of us.

The fruits of the Holy Spirit are love, joy, peace, longsuffering, gentleness, goodness, faith, Meekness, temperance. A saved man will have in him the Spirit of God and will have the fruits of the Holy Spirit. However, possession of these good qualities without accepting Jesus as "Lord" will not entail us eligible to secure eternal life.

The only way to have eternal life is to confess by mouth that Jesus is Lord, and believe in heart that God raised Him from the dead on the third day. Believe on the efficacy of the blood of Lord Jesus Christ and accept that He died in our stead on the cross and rose from the dead.

CHAPTER 16
DID JESUS NAIL LAW ON THE CROSS?

" Blotting out the handwriting of ordinances that was against us, which was contrary to us, and took it out of the way, nailing it to his cross" Colossians 2:14 (KJV)

There is a misunderstand that Jesus nailed the Law on the cross and abolished it. At the very start of His ministry on this earth, while preaching the Sermon on the Mount, as recorded in Matthew Chapters 5-7, Jesus made it very clear that He did not come to abolish the Law, but to fulfill it.

"Think not that I am come to destroy the law, or the prophets: I am not come to destroy, but to fulfil. For verily I say unto you, Till heaven and earth pass, one jot or one tittle shall in no wise pass from the law, till all be fulfilled" (Matthew 5:17-18)

If it so, what is that then Apostle Paul writes in Colossians 2:14?

An easier understanding of the verse is:

"having canceled the charge of our legal indebtedness, which stood against us and condemned us; he has taken it away, nailing it to the cross" Colossians 2:14 (NIV)

Or,

"by canceling the record of debt that stood against us with its legal demands. This he set aside, nailing it to the cross" Colossians 2:14 (ESV)

It is wrong notion that Jesus nailed the Law on the cross; no, He did not. Law surely pointed guilt of a person. By observing

Mosaic Law none of us can be saved. Salvation is by grace through faith.

What is achieved on the cross was not abolition of the Law or nailing of the Law on the cross, but the abolition of debts of sinners that stood against them. The legal demands of the Law were nailed to the cross and wiped out. In other words, Jesus set aside the record of these debts on the cross; it is this record that was abolished. If Jesus nailed the Law, it is equivalent of saying that Jesus failed in His mission.

In fact Jesus set us on higher plane of the Law to follow the demands of law, by saying that lusting after woman is equivalent to committing adultery. A man calling his brother "Raca", shall be in danger of the council; a man calling another "Thou fool, shall be in danger of hell fire".

At this rate none of us can be saved. It is all by the grace of God that saves us.

"But I say unto you, That whosoever is angry with his brother without a cause shall be in danger of the judgment: and whosoever shall say to his brother, Raca, shall be in danger of the council: but whosoever shall say, Thou fool, shall be in danger of hell fire". (Matthew 5:22)

Jews contented with Gentiles on one main reason that the latter did not keep the Law. There was physical barrier, the actual "wall of separation" between them, in the temple, separating Jew from Gentile.

The Gentiles were aliens to the commonwealth of Israel. By the blood of Jesus Christ offered on the cross He reconciled them together to make them "One New Man" in Christ. The finished work of Lord Jesus Christ on the cross is the reason for reconciling Jews with Gentiles. He brought them together. He did not abolish the Law, but fulfilled the law for this purpose, and this is the common ground for the salvation of Jews and Gentiles. No one could receive salvation by keeping the Law; but every sinner could be saved by believing in Jesus Christ, who canceled the list of our sins on the cross. (cf. Eph. 2:13,16)

"Christ hath redeemed us from the curse of the law, being made a curse for us: for it is written, Cursed is every one that hangeth on a tree" (Galatians 3:13)

"For he is our peace, who hath made both one, and hath broken down the middle wall of partition between us; Having abolished in his flesh the enmity, even the law of commandments contained in ordinances; for to make in himself of twain one new man, so making peace" (Ephesians 2:14-15)

CHAPTER 17
SEALED WITH THE PROMISE OF HOLY SPIRIT

In whom ye also trusted, after that ye heard the word of truth, the gospel of your salvation: in whom also after that ye believed, ye were sealed with that holy Spirit of promise, Which is the earnest of our inheritance until the redemption of the purchased possession, unto the praise of his glory. Wherefore I also, after I heard of your faith in the Lord Jesus, and love unto all the saints, Cease not to give thanks for you, making mention of you in my prayers; That the God of our Lord Jesus Christ, the Father of glory, may give unto you the spirit of wisdom and revelation in the knowledge of him: (Ephesians 1:13-17)

Seal is an embossed emblem legally securing the ownership and protection of the possession. Inasmuch as we, who have believed in Him are His possession, and the Scripture says believers are sealed with the Holy Spirit of promise until we are redeemed at resurrection, no one can pluck us out from His protection. The Seal He has put on us is a deposit guaranteeing our redemption unto resurrection and everlasting life.

When a legal document is sealed it becomes a property of someone who protects it from not only from the damage it might suffer but also from misappropriation and stealth by enemy.

The redemption secured of the purchased possession is for the praise of the glory of God. Apostle Paul wishes Grace and peace from God our Father and from the Lord Jesus Christ to the believers in Ephesus and says God has blessed us with all spiritual blessings in heavenly places in Christ.

After we have heard the Gospel of Jesus Christ and trusted in Him as our Savior we have a sure promise that we will be redeemed according to the hope and inheritance of everlasting life to be with the Lord forever and ever. It is an inheritance which is incorruptible and undefiled and unfading reserved for us.

"To an inheritance incorruptible, and undefiled, and that fadeth not away, reserved in heaven for you" (1 Peter 1:4)

The Father has blessed us according to His great mercy to a living hope through the resurrection of Lord Jesus Christ from among the dead. He has chosen us before the foundation of the world, in Jesus Christ that we should be holy and blameless before Him in love. We have redemption through the blood of Lord Jesus Christ.

The Scripture says in blood there is life and blood needs to be shed for the redemption. If only Jesus did not pay the price of our redemption by His blood, and not dying a substitutionary death, we would have perished. The confession part rests with us and unless we confess our sins and believe in Him that He is the Lord and He was raised by God on the third day of His death, we will have no salvation.

"But God commendeth his love toward us, in that, while we were yet sinners, Christ died for us" (Romans 5:8)

Bible says there is no one righteous and everyone has come short of the glory of God. The wages of sin is death but the gift of God is everlasting life. In Jesus we have forgiveness of our sins according to the riches of grace.

"For all have sinned, and come short of the glory of God" (Romans 3:23)

"For the wages of sin is death; but the gift of God is eternal life through Jesus Christ our Lord". (Romans 6:23)

We were dead in trespass and He died for us even when we were sinners. We walked according to the ways of the world, obeying the price of the power of the air, which is Satan, and the spirit now is at work in the children of disobedience (cf. Ephesians 2:2)

Ephesians 1:13-17 points to three phases.

1. Firstly, it is of our past stance in Christ, secondly of our present stance in Christ and thirdly of our future stance in Christ. We are sealed by the Holy Spirit of promise unto redemption when we believed. It is that seal which loudly proclaims that we are possession of our Lord Jesus Christ. He is our owner and if so, who can pluck us from His hands?
2. Secondly, in the present stance Holy Spirit gives us the "spirit of wisdom and revelation in the knowledge of him"
3. Thirdly, in the future after we are called home, we are redeemed of the present body made of dust, and the dead in Christ shall rise and those who are alive will rise and be caught up, and receive a glorified body in the twinkling of an eye when the Lord comes down from "heaven with a shout, with the voice of the archangel, and with the trump of God: and the dead in Christ shall

rise first: Then we which are alive and remain shall be caught up together with them in the clouds, to meet the Lord in the air: and so shall we ever be with the Lord". (1 Thessalonians 4:16-17)

Who can separate us from the love of God?

"Nor height, nor depth, nor any other creature, shall be able to separate us from the love of God, which is in Christ Jesus our Lord" (Romans 8:39)

Our future everlasting life is guaranteed by the promise of Holy Spirit who sealed us when we believed in Christ. He is our mediator between us and the Father. He died on behalf of us to redeem us from the transgressions in order that all those who are called might receive the promise of the eternal life (cf. Hebrews 9:15)

Inasmuch as Christ has delivered us from the bondage of sin, we have assurance that we are sealed unto redemption, unlike those that are not sealed and heading to be judged of their sins. It is, therefore, imperative that we grow in the spirit of wisdom and revelation of the knowledge of Lord Jesus Christ, we glorifying Him. Our focus now should be our daily life in Christ.

CHAPTER 18
BE GLAD IN THE LORD

"Be glad in the LORD, and rejoice, ye righteous: and shout for joy, all ye that are upright in heart" Psalm 32:11

David, having found grace in the sight of the LORD, comforts not only his soul, but of others as well. He asserts that blessed are those whose transgression is forgiven and whose sin is covered (cf. Psalms 32:1).

Indeed, he had good reasons to rejoice in the LORD because he was forgiven not only of his adultery with Hittite woman, Bathsheba but also for being the cause of the killing of her husband Uriah in the battle.

David's thoughts drifted from the path of righteousness when he, as a King, did not go into the battle-field to fight enemy; but stayed home and deliberately put Uriah in front in the battle field in order that he may get killed in the battle. And when he stayed home his eyes fell on Bathsheba who was taking bath in her home.

Except for the grace of God he had no chance of being blessed in his life.

What pleased God was that David repented of his sin and also obeyed the command of the LORD with regard to fully destroy the Amalekites. His predecessor, King Saul, on the contrary displeased the LORD because he did that which he should not have done. He was not a priest to offer sacrifices, but when Samuel delayed in coming for offer sacrifices, Saul took God's Law into his hands and offered sacrifices, In addition he did not obey fully the commandment of the LORD with regard to fully destroying the Amalekites resulting in his wisdom and priorities to rule over God's commandments, in spite of enjoying God's unflinching support from God.

"And the LORD sent thee on a journey, and said, Go and utterly destroy the sinners the Amalekites, and fight against them until they be consumed" (1 Samuel 15:18)

"And Samuel said unto Saul, I will not return with thee: for thou hast rejected the word of the LORD, and the LORD hath rejected thee from being king over Israel" (1 Samuel 15:26)

"For rebellion is as the sin of witchcraft, and stubbornness is as iniquity and idolatry. Because thou hast rejected the word of the LORD, he hath also rejected thee from being king" (1 Samuel 15:23)

God's commendation of David to blessed status is seen in Acts 13:22 where the LORD's words are that he was after the LORD's own heart.

"After removing Saul, he made David their king. God testified concerning him: 'I have found David son of Jesse, a man after my own heart; he will do everything I want him to do.'" Acts 13:22

David's procrastination in confessing his sin exceedingly troubled him in his heart, and he groaned many a day, the entire day. Day and night God's hand weighed very heavy on him, and his strength waxed weak. His health continually deteriorated as if water in his body evaporated due to the heat of the summer.

David knew that if he confessed his sins, the LORD does not hold them against him and he knew that God will not hold him responsible of his sins because he repented of his sin, and had no deceit in his heart. David's comfort arose from the decision he made that read "I will confess my transgressions to the Lord".

As soon as David acknowledged his sin before the LORD and refraining further from continuing to hide it from the LORD his guilt of sinning against the LOD was forgiven.

David, after receiving assurance of his salvation, desires that all the faithful may pray to the LORD, while he may be found. He seeks from others the same attitude of confessing their sins to the LORD.

The LORD is night unto them that seek Him and He is their shelter to hide them under His wings. He protects us from trouble and causes us to praise Him with songs of deliverance.

Therefore, David says a man should not be rebellious. The LORD will teach us the way we should tread on. The LORD gives us His counsel with His loving eye on us. He advises us not be like horse or as the mule that have no understanding but must be controlled with bit and bridle lest they hurt us.

Many are the afflictions of wicked, but the LORD is near to them that seek Him. There is reason for the righteous and upright in heart to rejoice in the Lord and be glad in Him and sing unto Him praises continually.

"Be ye not as the horse, or as the mule, which have no understanding: whose mouth must be held in with bit and bridle, lest they come near unto thee". Psalm 32:9

Jesus said:

"Come unto me, all ye that labour and are heavy laden, and I will give you rest". (Matthew 11:28)

CHAPTER 19
THE BRIDE

"What is thy beloved more than another beloved, O thou fairest among women? what is thy beloved more than another beloved, that thou dost so charge us? My beloved is white and ruddy, the chiefest among ten thousand" (Song of Solomon 5:9-10)

The bride waiting for her bridegroom describes him as the "chiefest among ten thousand". We would know the true meaning of the Church if we could appreciate the words of Adam when he saw the woman. The LORD God caused a deep sleep to fall upon Adam and when he was sleeping God took one of his ribs and closed up the flesh in its place. God made the rib of man a woman and brought the woman unto man.

"And Adam said, This is now bone of my bones, and flesh of my flesh: she shall be called Woman, because she was taken out of Man". (Genesis 2:23)

The word of God says:

"Therefore shall a man leave his father and his mother, and shall cleave unto his wife: and they shall be one flesh". (Genesis 2:24)

This glorious truth is presented to us by Apostle Paul in Ephesians 5:22-25

"Wives, submit yourselves unto your own husbands, as unto the Lord. For the husband is the head of the wife, even as Christ is the head of the church: and he is the saviour of the body. Therefore as the church is subject unto Christ, so let the wives be to their own husbands in every thing. Husbands, love your wives, even as Christ also loved the church, and gave himself for it" (Ephesians 5:22-25)

The relationship between the husband and the wife is that husband is the head of the wife, even as Christ is the head of the Church. Christ is the savior of the body and he presents to himself a bride that is holy and without blemish.

"That he might present it to himself a glorious church, not having spot, or wrinkle, or any such thing; but that it should be holy and without blemish". (Ephesians 5:27)

All those whose sin is cleansed by the blood of Christ are the members of the Church, which is the body of Christ.

"Now ye are the body of Christ, and members in particular". (1 Corinthians 12:27)

The church is the body of Christ with many members, whose head is Lord Jesus Christ. The church, which is a composition of members, just as the body is the composition of various parts, one member cannot say to any other member that former does not need the latter in the church, unless the latter is heretic indoctrinating other members; and needs to be corrected or a decision needs to be taken just as any part of the body that is rotten with incurable disease needs amputation; nevertheless, no action can be taken unless the method described in Matthew 18:15-20 is followed.

"Moreover if thy brother shall trespass against thee, go and tell him his fault between thee and him alone: if he shall hear thee, thou hast gained thy brother. But if he will not hear thee, then take with thee one or two more, that in the mouth of two or

three witnesses every word may be established. And if he shall neglect to hear them, tell it unto the church: but if he neglect to hear the church, let him be unto thee as an heathen man and a publican. Verily I say unto you, Whatsoever ye shall bind on earth shall be bound in heaven: and whatsoever ye shall loose on earth shall be loosed in heaven. Again I say unto you, That if two of you shall agree on earth as touching any thing that they shall ask, it shall be done for them of my Father which is in heaven. For where two or three are gathered together in my name, there am I in the midst of them" (Matthew 18:15-20)

The body of Christ is baptized by one Spirit irrespective of whether the members are Jews or Gentiles, or bond or free. One part of the body cannot say to the other that it has no need of the other. Foot cannot call itself separate from the body because it is not hand, nor can eye can call itself separate because it is not ear, nor can any body part say to the other that it has no need of the other part (cf. 1 Corinthians 12:12-24).

The whole body suffers if one of its members suffers loss or damage.

Church is not a building or simply a called out people, or congregation, or gathering of citizens, or social gathering, or discussion or debating forum. It is not also the "kingdom of God". The Church is the "Body of Christ". The Church is the "Bride of Christ" waiting for the bridegroom to come and take her.

Careful observation of Ephesians Chapter 5 gives us the answer that the one who is presenting to Himself is Lord Jesus Christ and He is presenting to Himself a glorious Church that has no spot, or wrinkle of any such thing. Lord Jesus Christ is expecting from the Church that the church should be without blemish.

The one, who was described by the bride as the "My beloved is white and ruddy, the chiefest among ten thousand" became "as a root out of a dry ground: he hath no form nor comeliness; and when we shall see him, there is no beauty that we should desire him. He is despised and rejected of men; a man of sorrows, and acquainted with grief: and we hid as it were our faces from him; he was despised, and we esteemed him not" for our sake when He was crucified on the cross. It is all for you and me!

"For he shall grow up before him as a tender plant, and as a root out of a dry ground: he hath no form nor comeliness; and when we shall see him, there is no beauty that we should desire him. He is despised and rejected of men; a man of sorrows, and acquainted with grief: and we hid as it were our faces from him; he was despised, and we esteemed him not". (Isaiah 53:2-3)

The Lord is not in the grave today; but He is alive, and we have victory in Him. Apostle Peter testifies about Him this way...

"Ye men of Israel, hear these words; Jesus of Nazareth, a man approved of God among you by miracles and wonders and signs, which God did by him in the midst of you, as ye yourselves also know: Him, being delivered by the determinate counsel and foreknowledge of God, ye have taken, and by wicked hands have crucified and slain: Whom God hath raised up, having loosed the pains of death: because it was not possible that he should be holden of it". (Acts 2:22-24)

HE IS OUR HIGH PRIEST

"For we have not an high priest which cannot be touched with the feeling of our infirmities; but was in all points tempted like as we are, yet without sin. Let us therefore come boldly unto the throne of grace, that we may obtain mercy, and find grace to help in time of need" (Hebrews 4:15-16)

"For such an high priest became us, who is holy, harmless, undefiled, separate from sinners, and made higher than the heavens" (Hebrews 7:26)

Then Samuel took a stone and set it up between Mizpah and Shen and called its name Ebenezer; for he said, "Till now the LORD has helped us" 1 Samuel 7:12

Samuel the prophet was the last judge in Israel before Saul was made king by God over Israel. The people prospered and were blessed when there was theocracy, i.e. when they were under the direct rule of God. However, soon they drifted into worshipping strange gods and Ashtaroth and God's anger was kindled against them.

There was a situation when Samuel had to be very tough with the children of Israel and said to them to put away strange gods and Ashtaroth from among them and get ready to serve the LORD only and none else. He promised them that if they obey the LORD, He will deliver them from the hands of Philistines. Samuel's intervention prevailed and the children of Israel put away Baalim and Ashtaroth and served the LORD only. The children of Israel repented and said "We have sinned against the LORD".

When the lords of philistines went against the children of Israel to fight them down they said to Samuel to intercede with the LORD on behalf of them to save them from the hand of Philistines. Samuel offered burnt offering to the LORD and the LORD heard him. As Samuel was interceding with the LORD philistines drew near to battle against them; but the LORD's mighty thunder discomfited them and they were smitten before the children of Israel.

Then Samuel pronounced saying, "Hitherto hath the LORD helped us". The LORD helped the children of Israel even as they fell into idol worship and turned to the LORD and after every fall and rise they acknowledged "Till now the LORD has helped us."

"So the Philistines were subdued, and they came no more into the coast of Israel: and the hand of the LORD was against the Philistines all the days of Samuel" (1 Samuel 7:13)

Samuel's intercession is seen here. People repented. They won the battle against Philistines and erected a stone to remember their victory. Samuel acknowledged God's help and said "Till now the LORD has helped us."

As the children of Israel went up to Jerusalem three times a year to worship the LORD they sang...

"I lift up my eyes to the hills. From where does my help come? My help comes from the LORD, who made heaven and earth" (Psalm 121:1-2 ESV)

Yes, indeed where our help comes from? Our help comes from the LORD who gave His only Son, Lord Jesus Christ, for our sake that whoever believes in Him shall not perish but have everlasting life; and no doubt, wc will then be able to say...

"Till now the LORD has helped us"

Lord Jesus Christ is our high priest, who is not insensitive to our afflictions, but is sympathetic to us; therefore we can boldly approach Him to find grace and to seek His help in time of our need. He was tempted just as any of us, and yet without sin. He was without any blemish and He was perfect. In His incarnation He became poor for our sake, He dwelt among us, He was despised, He was scourged and suffered pain on behalf us.

"Who did no sin, neither was guile found in his mouth" (1 Peter 2:22)

"For he hath made him to be sin for us, who knew no sin; that we might be made the righteousness of God in him" (2 Corinthians 5:21)

Although He did well for mankind, healed the sick, cast away demons from those who possessed evil spirts, people persecuted Him. He was tempted by the devil but the Lord was triumphant in all circumstances. He became sin for us in order that whoever accepts Him as Lord by confessing their sins to Him and believes in heart that God raised Him from the dead will have salvation free of cost.

"That if thou shalt confess with thy mouth the Lord Jesus, and shalt believe in thine heart that God hath raised him from the dead, thou shalt be saved" (Romans 10:9)

CHAPTER 20
TIME IS FLEETING

"Redeeming the time, because the days are evil" (Ephesians 5:16)

Time neither stops nor can be stopped by anyone. However wise or mighty one may be, the time has advantage over a lazy or unfruitful man. The wisest man on the earth, King Solomon wrote:

"The ants are a people not strong, yet they prepare their meat in the summer; The conies are but a feeble folk, yet make they their houses in the rocks; The locusts have no king, yet go they forth all of them by bands; The spider taketh hold with her hands, and is in kings' palaces" (Proverbs 30:25-28)

Many of us indeed feel sorry for having lost much time on discussing trivial matters of celebrities, or engaging in frivolous discussions, or turning the pages of newspapers to read articles of base and mean things of life.

Bible exhorts believers to redeem the time because the days are evil. Redeem the time as and when it is available, seize the opportunity to preach the Gospel of Jesus Christ because the days are evil.

It is the best way to do good to all men, especially to those who are already believers because they need to be refreshed in their knowledge of the truth in order for them to preach the Gospel of Jesus Christ. The days are evil and none of us can afford to waste our time.

What does it mean to redeem the time? It is buying back or rescuing something that was lost. Bible exhorts us that we, who are born-again, were once in darkness, but now as we are in the light, we should walk as the children of light. When the light shines all the things of the darkness are exposed.

Therefore the Lord says that the children of God should arise from ineptitude and be awake to the knowledge of the truth. The Lord says that we should walk circumspectly, not as fools, but as wise redeeming the time because the days we live now are full of evil.

"Even when we were dead in sins, hath quickened us together with Christ, (by grace ye are saved ;)" (Ephesians 2:5)

The concept of redemption was seen in Leviticus 25:23-27; Ruth 4:4 and in many more passages. The substitutionary sacrifice was best described in Genesis 22:8-14.

Lord Jesus became sweet-smelling aroma before the Father, by offering Himself as sacrifice on the cross by laying down his life as substitution on behalf of us to buy back us from the penalty of death, by paying not silver or gold, but by paying His precious blood. We were lost and dead in trespasses once, but He redeemed us from the bondage of sin to give us eternal life. It was the only way available to redeem us from eternal punishment.

The children of God are exhorted to show love towards not only one to another but even to enemies. It was the love similar to that the Lord showed towards those who killed Him on the cross that He wants believers to show.

Stephen, who was human, just as we are, showed such love, when he was stoned to death. His assertion when he was breathing his last was similar to the assertion of Jesus who said "Father forgive them for they do not know what they do"

"...Father, forgive them; for they know not what they do..."

"And be ye kind one to another, tenderhearted, forgiving one another, even as God for Christ's sake hath forgiven you" (Ephesians 4:32)

A sinner can become child of God by confessing his/her sins to Jesus and by accepting Him as personal savior.

It is not fitting for the children of God to resort to fornication, or any uncleanness or covetousness, filthiness, foolish talking, coarse jesting as they all belong to the sons of disobedience and they face God's wrath. The point of focus here was on 'foolish talking', and 'coarse jesting' which are in essence the turning every conversation into joking, and ending up in talks about sexual matters.

"But as he which hath called you is holy, so be ye holy in all manner of conversation; Because it is written, Be ye holy; for I am holy" (1 Peter 1:15-16)

Bible asks us to thank "God and the Father in the name of our Lord Jesus Christ" for the goodness He has shown to us, and the loving relationship of Christ with the church.

It pleased the Father to bruise His one and only Son on the cross to redeem us from the bondage of sin that by confessing by mouth that Jesus is Lord and God raised Him from the dead one can have everlasting life and be conformed to the image of Jesus when He comes in the clouds.

"Yet it pleased the LORD to bruise him; he hath put him to grief: when thou shalt make his soul an offering for sin, he shall see his seed, he shall prolong his days, and the pleasure of the LORD shall prosper in his hand" (Isaiah 53:10)

"For the Lord himself shall descend from heaven with a shout, with the voice of the archangel, and with the trump of God: and the dead in Christ shall rise first: Then we which are alive and remain shall be caught up together with them in the clouds, to meet the Lord in the air: and so shall we ever be with the Lord" (1 Thessalonians 4:16-17)

As we have therefore opportunity, let us do good unto all men, especially unto them who are of the household of faith. (Galatians 6:10)

CHAPTER 21
UNSEARCHABLE RICHES IN CHRIST

The unsearchable riches of Christ that Paul taught were similar to the unsearchable depths of the sea, the limits of which cannot be accurately measured. Those riches in Christ were the provision of salvation to Gentiles and their status being considered on par with the Jews.

THE MYSTERY REVEALED

It is the Church age and it was a mystery in the Old Testament period. It was revealed to Apostle Paul by Lord Jesus Christ, and the mystery revealed was that "the Gentiles should be fellowheirs, and of the same body, and partakers of his promise in Christ by the gospel" (Ephesians 3:2-6)

Paul writes...

"If ye have heard of the dispensation of the grace of God which is given me to you-ward: How that by revelation he made known unto me the mystery; (as I wrote afore in few words, Whereby, when ye read, ye may understand my knowledge in the mystery of Christ) Which in other ages was not made known unto the sons of men, as it is now revealed unto his holy apostles and prophets by the Spirit; That the Gentiles should be fellowheirs, and of the same body, and partakers of his promise in Christ by the gospel" (Ephesians 3:2-6)

Barnabas, who was also sent forth to preach the Gospel of Jesus Christ, brought Paul to the apostles and "declared unto them how he had seen the Lord in the way, and that he had spoken to him, and how he had preached boldly at Damascus in the name of Jesus". (cf. Acts 9:27; 11:22)

It is that reason that Paul says he was given the responsibility of preaching the unsearchable riches in Christ to the Gentiles. It is this office of an apostle that was given to him of which he mentions in Ephesians 3:8-11

BY GOD'S GRACE

"Unto me, who am less than the least of all saints, is this grace given, that I should preach among the Gentiles the unsearchable riches of Christ; And to make all men see what is the fellowship of the mystery, which from the beginning of the world hath been hid in God, who created all things by Jesus Christ: To the intent that now unto the principalities and powers in heavenly places might be known by the church the manifold wisdom of God, According to the eternal purpose which he purposed in Christ Jesus our Lord" (Ephesians 3:8-11)

THE CITY OF NEW JERUSALEM

"And had a wall great and high, and had twelve gates, and at the gates twelve angels, and names written thereon, which are the names of the twelve tribes of the children of Israel" (Revelation 21:12)

The city in itself will be so beautiful that there will be no temple in it, and no ordinary light that we currently see. But "the Lord God Almighty and the Lamb are the temple of it" and "the glory of God did lighten it, and the Lamb is the light thereof"

"And I saw no temple therein: for the Lord God Almighty and the Lamb are the temple of it. And the city had no need of the sun, neither of the moon, to shine in it: for the glory of God did lighten it, and the Lamb is the light thereof". (Revelation 21:22-23)

"And the foundations of the wall of the city were garnished with all manner of precious stones. The first foundation was jasper; the second, sapphire; the third, a chalcedony; the fourth, an emerald; The fifth, sardonyx; the sixth, sardius; the seventh, chrysolite; the eighth, beryl; the ninth, a topaz; the tenth, a chrysoprasus; the eleventh, a jacinth; the twelfth, an amethyst. And the twelve gates were twelve pearls; every several gate was of one pearl: and the street of the city was pure gold, as it were transparent glass" (Revelation 21:19-21)

THE FOUNDATION LAID

"And are built upon the foundation of the apostles and prophets, Jesus Christ himself being the chief corner stone" (Ephesians 2:20)

The Church is not a building but it constitutes believers in the Christ. In the Old Testament period God came and dwelt in the Tabernacle and in the Temple and therefore, the church is often compared with a building in the New Testament.

Apostle Paul speaks of the church which is firmly founded on the apostolic doctrines, and the prophets, whose corner stone, is Lord Jesus Christ. He also wrote that the Church is the body of Christ, whose head is Jesus Christ. Also the Church is compared as the bride whose marriage with the Lord takes place in heaven and marriage feast on the earth.

When it comes to laying the foundation of the church the work was already done and complete. No more foundation is required because never a foundation is laid on another foundation. The church grows, and expands until the second advent of Lord Jesus Christ.

APOSTLE

The literal meaning of "apostle" is "one sent forth," an envoy, missionary. The followers of the teachings of Lord Jesus grew greatly in number before Apostle Paul commenced his ministry for the Lord. Saul, who was called Paul, was terribly persecuting the followers of Jesus, but very quickly stopped by the Lord calling Him to be an apostle to preach the Gospel of Jesus Christ to the Gentiles.

The commission given by Lord Jesus Christ as it is written in Matthew 28:16-20, commenced officially only after the commission given in Acts 1:8 was put into practice. The disciples of Jesus Christ preached the Gospel of Jesus Christ even before Apostle Paul preached.

Apostle Paul was a great instrument in the hands of God to reveal the mystery of the Church and provision of salvation to the Gentiles. Fourteen books (including Hebrews), which form the chunk of the New Testament, are written by him.

PROPHET

The Biblical definition of 'Prophet' is that if the prophecy spoken by him in the name of the LORD does not come to pass, then he is not a prophet, but if the word spoken by him in the name of the LORD comes to pass, then he is a prophet of God.

"When a prophet speaketh in the name of the LORD, if the thing follow not, nor come to pass, that is the thing which the LORD hath not spoken, but the prophet hath spoken it presumptuously: thou shalt not be afraid of him" (Deuteronomy 18:22)

CHAPTER 22
WHAT IS MAN TO BE MINDFUL OF?

"But one in a certain place testified, saying, What is man, that thou art mindful of him? or the son of man, that thou visitest him? Thou madest him a little lower than the angels; thou crownedst him with glory and honour, and didst set him over the works of thy hands" (Hebrews 2:6-7)

The shepherd boy David, who was later anointed as King over Israel, was so elegant in his poetic and truthful assertion, of the beauty of milky galaxy that no one, who reads Psalm 8, would miss the prophetical musings in it albeit he was mentioning of his own status.

After he saw the beauty of the sun, moon and the stars, he finds himself as humble being as one who is lower than the angels in creation. Angels are ministering spirits, and yet inasmuch as they can attain any form, and are not constrained by the physical body, they are superior in creation over men, whose soul is bound within the physical body structure.

At the death of man the conscience of man is separated from the body, but in the case of believer, he is never spiritually dead. He is always with the Lord moving out from this earthly tabernacle, into eternal state in Him. (cf. 1 Corinthians 15:16, Phil. 3:21).

"For we know that if our earthly house of this tabernacle were dissolved, we have a building of God, an house not made with hands, eternal in the heavens". (2 Corinthians 5:1)

Christ defeated death and because He defeated Satan, who brought in death, we will be victorious in our resurrection. When the Lord comes again we will rise and say to the grave "where is thy victory?", and those, who are "caught up" will say "O death, where is thy sting?"

"O death, where is thy sting? O grave, where is thy victory? The sting of death is sin; and the strength of sin is the law" (1 Corinthians 15:55-56)

The writer of the book of Hebrews brings home this point while quoting from Psalm 8 that man is made little lower than the angels, and in order to redeem man from the bondage of sin, Jesus, the "Son of God" had to become, for a certain period of time, little lower than angels.

Jesus, the Son of God, who took upon Himself our sin died for our sake, and He was raised by God on the third day. This is the mystery of Triune God, who exists as the Father, the Son and the Holy Spirit. It pleased the Father to bruise His Son on the cross for our sake that we might believe in Him and live eternally.

After God has created everything in heaven, on earth and in the seas, He made man a ruler and authority over his creation. The LORD crowned him with glory and honor, and set him over the works of His hands, by saying,

"...Be fruitful, and multiply, and replenish the earth, and subdue it: and have dominion over the fish of the sea, and over the fowl of the air, and over every living thing that moveth upon the earth" (Genesis 1:28)

Man is made of dust of the earth and yet He loved him so much that the LORD visited him and had fellowship with him in the Garden of Eden. It was an honor more than an earthly king would visit a laborer in his regime and dine with him.

However, Satan by his cunning art in speech, deceived Adam and Eve and stole away not only the earth from him, but also authority from him. It took the "Son of God" to come to this earth, by becoming like man in the likeness of man and die for man that man may have everlasting life by accepting Jesus as personal savior.

CHAPTER 23
PROUD HE KNOWETH AFAR OFF

"Though the LORD be high, yet hath he respect unto the lowly: but the proud he knoweth afar off" (Psalms 138:6)

This meditation is about two individuals in the war between Philistines and the children of Israel at a land that belonged to Judah. The first one was Goliath, who was proud, huge, tall, strong man from Philistines. The second one was David, the son of Jesse, who belonged to the children of Israel.

Philistines took pride in their leader Goliath in the battle at Shochloh, which belonged to Judah. Saul and men of Israel gathered on the other side by the valley of Elah. Philistines stood on a mountain on one side and the Israel stood on a mountain on the other side (1 Samuel 17:1-3)

Saul was the first king of Israel. He was the son of Kish from the tribe of Benjamin. He was young, handsome and taller than any one among the children of Israel. (1 Samuel 9:1-2)

There was no response to Goliath's challenge either from Saul or any one from Israel until the ruddy shepherd David came along to take up the challenge. Goliath looked upon David with scorn and shouted. Goliath ridiculed the God of Israel and wondered if David thought that Goliath was a dog! He boasted in his gods and said that he would give David's flesh to the fowls of the air and to the beasts of the field.

The response from David who hoped in the Almighty and living God was equally challenging. David honored the living God when he said to Goliath that he was facing the mighty man in the name of the Lord of hosts, the God of armies of Israel, whom Goliath defied.

"Then said David to the Philistine, Thou comest to me with a sword, and with a spear, and with a shield: but I come to thee in the name of the LORD of hosts, the God of the armies of Israel, whom thou hast defied. This day will the LORD deliver thee into mine hand; and I will smite thee, and take thine head from thee; and I will give the carcases of the host of the Philistines this day unto the fowls of the air, and to the wild beasts of the earth; that all the earth may know that there is a God in Israel". (1 Samuel 17:45-46)

Goliath arose, went to meet David in the battlefield, and drew close, like a stalking mountain, overlaid with brass and iron. David advanced with greater strength in God and cheerfulness, as one that aimed more to execute God's command rather than to make a figure: He hasted, and ran, was being lightly clad, to meet the Philistine. Before honor is humility.

David put one of the pebbles in the sling and hurled at Goliath. There it was! The pebble struck straight at Goliath's forehead and in the twinkling of an eye, it fetched him to the ground. Goliath fell with his face down on the ground.

"Therefore David ran, and stood upon the Philistine, and took his sword, and drew it out of the sheath thereof, and slew him, and cut off his head therewith. And when the Philistines saw their champion was dead, they fled". (1 Samuel 17:51)

CHAPTER 24
PAY HEED TO THE LORD

"Therefore we ought to give the more earnest heed to the things which we have heard, lest at any time we should let them slip" (Hebrews 2:1)

Hebrews chapter 1 verse 1 starts with the word "Therefore". That is to say that there was, in the previous chapter, a very relevant subject on which the verses in this chapter are constructed.

Indeed, it was seen that there was considerable proof provided in chapter 1 of the superiority of Jesus over the angels. If so, then we ought to give more earnest heed to the things that we heard.

In addition to what Hebrews says about Jesus, who is superior to angels, and every human being, John the Baptist, who was forerunner of Jesus (not the Gospel writer John) bears witness of Jesus and says that of Him did He spoke that He who comes after him was preferred before Him, because He was before John, and of His fulness we all received grace for grace.

John continues saying that the Law was given by Moses, but the grace and truth came by Lord Jesus. He says that no man has seen God at any time, but the only begotten Son, Lord Jesus Christ, who was in the bosom of the Father, declared Him. (cf. John 1:15-18, John 1:29)

Next day, John the Baptist says that Jesus was the Lamb of God, who takes away the sin of the world Lord Jesus says...

"All things are delivered unto me of my Father: and no man knoweth the Son, but the Father; neither knoweth any man the Father, save the Son, and he to whomsoever the Son will reveal him. Come unto me, all ye that labour and are heavy laden and I will give you rest". (Matthew 11:27-28)

Inasmuch as Lord Jesus is above all, whether it be of all angels, or any human, the Word of God says to give more earnest heed to His sayings to avoid being slipped into evil or worldly errors.

It is easy for a believer to get distracted to the pleasures of this world. Keeping idle without pondering over the word of God, and without spending time in worshipping the Lord and in prayer will drift believers into carnal desires very soon.

When Jesus showed His glory to the innermost three disciples during transfiguration on the mountain, Moses and Elijah appeared and were talking to Him.

Peter, as impetuous as he was always, compared Lord Jesus with Moses and Elijah and said to the Lord that they may build tabernacles, one for the Lord, second one for Moses, and the third for Elijah.

However, as he was speaking a bright cloud overshadowed them and said "This is my beloved Son, in whom I am well pleased; hear ye him" When the disciples heard the voice "they fell on their face, and were sore afraid". (cf. Matthew 17:1-6)

It lays the emphasis that we should pay heed to the Lord's words rather than anybody else's. There is a clear warning that if we drift our ways or keep ourselves idle without doing anything for Him, we would slip from the righteous path and end up in darkness and in evil ways of the world. The words that

He spoke are spirit and life and He is the way the truth and the life (cf. John 6:63, John 14:6).

CHAPTER 25
HARDEN NOT YOUR HEARTS

"Therefore, as the Holy Spirit says, "Today, if you hear his voice, do not harden your hearts as in the rebellion, on the day of testing in the wilderness, where your fathers put me to the test and saw my works for forty years. Therefore I was provoked with that generation, and said, 'They always go astray in their heart; they have not known my ways.' As I swore in my wrath, 'They shall not enter my rest.'" (Hebrews 3:7-11 ESV)

Inspired by the Holy Spirit the writer of the book of Hebrews warns of the serious consequences of rebelling against God and neglecting to pay heed to His words. The children of Israel had already faced dire consequences and they were glaring examples for us to correct our attitude before the LORD.

The children of Israel murmured against God several times and tried to prove if He is able to deliver them from trivial things such as lack of food and water in the wilderness forgetting their great deliverance from slavery under Pharaoh of Egypt for four hundred years.

"Because all those men which have seen my glory, and my miracles, which I did in Egypt and in the wilderness, and have tempted me now these ten times, and have not hearkened to my voice" (Numbers 14:22)

The phrase "ten times" may mean to some exact ten times, but it is a metaphor used to signify frequent rebellion. God promised them rest in the Promised Land flowing with milk and honey and led them through the Red sea by parting into two, and drowning their enemy Pharaoh and his chariots in the waters of the Red Sea.

For those in the New Testament period the words of Lord Jesus Christ that we should "first the Kingdom of God and all these things shall be added unto you" are so comforting, yet just as the children of Israel murmured against God we too murmur against God several times.

"But seek ye first the kingdom of God, and his righteousness; and all these things shall be added unto you" (Matthew 6:33)

"Jesus answered and said unto him, Verily, verily, I say unto thee, Except a man be born again, he cannot see the kingdom of God" (John 3:3)

God created the heavens and the earth and all that is therein, yet we stumble at His promises many a time. Many times our attitude towards God shows that we are no better than the children of Israel, who complained against their leader Moses and rebelled against God.

The writer of Hebrew quotes the writing of Psalmist corroborating to the fact that the Scriptures are true and every word of the Bible is so precious. Psalmist refers to the rebellion of the children of Israel that the LORD was grieved with them for forty years. They did not have strong faith in the LORD that He will be able to provide all their needs and lead them through any trying situation.

It is because of their fall and rising and falling again repeatedly that the LORD said to them that they will not enter into His rest. (cf. Numbers 14:28-35). All those, except for Joshua the son of Nun, and Caleb the son of Jephunneh, who left Egypt for

Canaan perished in the wilderness. Only those children born in the wilderness entered in the Promised Land.

What is this "rest" that the LORD was referring to? Does it mean taking rest from everything in life and take rest or rest in heaven or something else?

The word "rest" in the case of the children of Israel refers to their entry into the Promised Land flowing with milk and honey, and in the case of the New Testament believer it refers to entering into the peaceful spiritual realm to walk in newness of life.

"Therefore we are buried with him by baptism into death: that like as Christ was raised up from the dead by the glory of the Father, even so we also should walk in newness of life". (Romans 6:4)

"But if the Spirit of him that raised up Jesus from the dead dwell in you, he that raised up Christ from the dead shall also quicken your mortal bodies by his Spirit that dwelleth in you" (Romans 8:11)

It is the eternal salvation gained by grace through faith in Lord Jesus Christ. It is the peace of God that He said He will give it to us. It is the LORD's rest and it is that rest that God promised to give to us. It is so true that those hardening their hearts, and seeking salvation by their own methods, will not enter into His rest. No method other than accepting Jesus as the Lord and believing that God raised Him from the dead will help anyone enter into His rest.

"Peace I leave with you, my peace I give unto you: not as the world giveth, give I unto you. Let not your heart be troubled, neither let it be afraid" (John 14:27)

The writer of Hebrews writes, as also Psalmist wrote that the believers' position in Him will be so pleasant and peaceful if only they do not harden their hearts "today" is applicable for any generation and any day they read the Scriptures.

"For he is our God; and we are the people of his pasture, and the sheep of his hand. To day if ye will hear his voice, Harden not your heart, as in the provocation, and as in the day of temptation in the wilderness: When your fathers tempted me, proved me, and saw my work. Forty years long was I grieved with this generation, and said, It is a people that do err in their heart, and they have not known my ways: Unto whom I sware in my wrath that they should not enter into my rest" (Psalms 95:7-11)

"Say unto them, As truly as I live, saith the LORD, as ye have spoken in mine ears, so will I do to you: Your carcasses shall fall in this wilderness; and all that were numbered of you, according to your whole number, from twenty years old and upward, which have murmured against me, Doubtless ye shall not come into the land, concerning which I sware to make you dwell therein, save Caleb the son of Jephunneh, and Joshua the son of Nun. But your little ones, which ye said should be a prey, them will I bring in, and they shall know the land which ye have despised. But as for you, your carcasses, they shall fall in this wilderness" (Numbers 14:28-32)

CHAPTER 26
HOW SHALL WE ESCAPE?

"For if the word spoken by angels was steadfast, and every transgression and disobedience received a just recompense of reward; How shall we escape, if we neglect so great salvation; which at the first began to be spoken by the Lord, and was confirmed unto us by them that heard him; God also bearing them witness, both with signs and wonders, and with divers miracles, and gifts of the Holy Ghost, according to his own will?" (Hebrews 2:2-4)

The shortest explanation for the three verses cited above is that in contrast to the stringent method that was available for covering the sin of transgressor in the Old Testament period, the salvation provided by Lord Jesus Christ by grace through faith is so great that we cannot neglect it.

However, that does not suffice our need to clearly understand the concept of salvation because of the depth of knowledge available in these verses. Therefore, let us look into little more in detail.

The Ten Commandments were indeed written by God with His fingers. However, the disposition of the Law among the various ranks and files was made by angels. Stephen in his speech in Acts 7:38 and in Acts 7:53 and Paul in Galatians 3:19 confirm this fact.

The Mosaic Law pointed to the transgression and disobedience of the Law and the expiation to cover the sin was a very tough, and yet it was the beginning of the things to come, and it was the way to show that the sacrifice of Lord Jesus was perfect one. If such method was not available we would not have appreciated the greatness of Lord Jesus, who paid ransom for our sin, to deliver us from the bondage of sin.

The sacrifices offered on the altar in the prescribed manner by the Levite Priests were enough only for the sin of transgressor to be covered temporarily and it was never fully forgiven in the Old Testament period, until the price of it was fully paid by Lord Jesus on the cross by shedding His precious blood.

The Law was very severe, and it subjected everyone to suffer for every transgression and disobedience.

"But the person who does anything with a high hand, whether he is native or a sojourner, reviles the LORD, and that person shall be cut off from among his people. Because he has despised the word of the LORD and has broken his commandment, that person shall be utterly cut off; his iniquity shall be on him." (Numbers 15:30-31 ESV. cf. also Deuteronomy 17:12, Psalm 19:13, Hebrews 10:26).

Angels looked with great curiosity of this great salvation that we benefit from, while the prophets diligently searched to know what it was, and yet this mystery was revealed unto us. No one understood it fully until Jesus died on the cross and was raised from the dead.

The sacrifices offered by slaying thousands of animals was once for all replaced by the one and only sacrifice made by One Lord, One Christ, the divine being, who came into this world in the form of servant and in the likeness of man and dwelt among men.

The word spoken by angels was not vacillating or wavering but it was steadfast. Every transgression and disobedience received due recompense of reward. The way to permanent salvation came by grace through faith in Lord Jesus Christ.

That is the reason why the Word of God asks us how we can neglect this great salvation that we received. It is hard to increase in knowledge unless we work hard in that direction, but for degeneration of our body and brain, it is enough if we neglect the word of God.

A physical body needs continual upkeep; otherwise it stinks, a land needs continual upkeep; otherwise, weeds will surely grow in it. Our degeneration and backsliding occurs when we neglect our salvation.

No truly born-again child of God forsakes salvation once it is received, but every Christian undergoes severe trials and temptations in this life.

Our progress in the Lord increases only when we do not neglect the gift of salvation we received, and continually depend on Him seeing His guidance. The Lord calls all those who backslide to return to Him.

The forgiveness of sins in fully be achieved only by accepting Jesus as personal savior. He offered Himself on the cross as sacrifice on behalf of us that whoever believes in Him shall not perish but have everlasting life. Our salvation is secured by the Lord, and will, therefore, never be lost.

He took our sin upon Him and died a substitutionary death on behalf of us, in order that we by confessing Him as Lord and believing in heart that God raised Him from the dead on the third day might receive salvation, free of cost. The price is already paid by the Lord, not in the form of silver or gold but by His precious blood.

How can we escape if we neglect such great salvation afforded to us by God. We were not worthy to come to His feet, but He made us worthy to call Him as "Abba, Father". He gave us the privilege to be called as "sons of God".

The salvation that the Lord spoke of was confirmed to us by them that heard Him. God bore witness, both of signs and wonders and with various miracles, and gifts of the Holy Spirit, according to His will.

CHAPTER 27
BE GLAD IN THE LORD

"Be glad in the LORD, and rejoice, ye righteous: and shout for joy, all ye that are upright in heart" Psalm 32:11

David, having found grace in the sight of the LORD, comforts not only his soul, but of others as well. He asserts that blessed are those whose transgression is forgiven and whose sin is covered (cf. Psalms 32:1).

Indeed, he had good reasons to rejoice in the LORD because he was forgiven not only of his adultery with Hittite woman, Bathsheba but also for being the cause of the killing of her husband Uriah in the battle.

David's thoughts drifted from the path of righteousness when he, as a King, did not go into the battle field to fight enemy; but stayed home and deliberately put Uriah in front in the battle field in order that he may get killed in the battle. And when he stayed home his eyes fell on Bathsheba who was taking bath in her home. Except for the grace of God he had no chance of being blessed in his life.

What pleased God was that David repented of his sin and also obeyed the command of the LORD with regard to fully destroy the Amalekites. His predecessor, King Saul, on the contrary displeased the LORD because he did that which he should not have done. He was not a priest to offer sacrifices, but when Samuel delayed in coming for offer sacrifices, Saul took God's Law into his hands and offered sacrifices, In addition he did not obey fully the commandment of the LORD with regard to fully destroying the Amalekites resulting in his wisdom and priorities to rule over God's commandments, in spite of enjoying God's unflinching support from God.

"And the LORD sent thee on a journey, and said, Go and utterly destroy the sinners the Amalekites, and fight against them until they be consumed" (1 Samuel 15:18)

"And Samuel said unto Saul, I will not return with thee: for thou hast rejected the word of the LORD, and the LORD hath rejected thee from being king over Israel" (1 Samuel 15:26)

"For rebellion is as the sin of witchcraft, and stubbornness is as iniquity and idolatry. Because thou hast rejected the word of the LORD, he hath also rejected thee from being king" (1 Samuel 15:23)

God's commendation of David to blessed status is seen in Acts 13:22 where the LORD's words are that he was after the LORD's own heart.

"After removing Saul, he made David their king. God testified concerning him: 'I have found David son of Jesse, a man after my own heart; he will do everything I want him to do.'" Acts 13:22

David's procrastination in confessing his sin exceedingly troubled him in his heart, and he groaned many a day, the entire day. Day and night God's hand weighed very heavy on him, and his strength waxed weak. His health continually deteriorated as if water in his body evaporated due to the heat of the summer.

David knew that if he confessed his sins, the LORD does not hold them against him and he knew that God will not hold him responsible of his sins because he repented of his sin, and had no deceit in his heart. David's comfort arose from the decision he made that read "I will confess my transgressions to the Lord".

As soon as David acknowledged his sin before the LORD and refraining further from continuing to hide it from the LORD his guilt of sinning against the LOD was forgiven.

David, after receiving assurance of his salvation, desires that all the faithful may pray to the LORD, while he may be found. He seeks from others the same attitude of confessing their sins to the LORD.

The LORD is night unto them that seek Him and He is their shelter to hide them under His wings. He protects us from trouble and causes us to praise Him with songs of deliverance.

Therefore, David says a man should not be rebellious. The LORD will teach us the way we should tread on. The LORD gives us His counsel with His loving eye on us. He advises us not be like horse or as the mule that have no understanding but must be controlled with bit and bridle lest they hurt us.

Many are the afflictions of wicked, but the LORD is near to them that seek Him. There is reason for the righteous and upright in heart to rejoice in the Lord and be glad in Him and sing unto Him praises continually.

"Be ye not as the horse, or as the mule, which have no understanding: whose mouth must be held in with bit and bridle, lest they come near unto thee". Psalm 32:9

Jesus said:

"Come unto me, all ye that labour and are heavy laden, and I will give you rest". (Matthew 11:28)

CHAPTER 28
SIN SHALL NOT HAVE DOMINION

"And God is able to make all grace abound toward you; that ye, always having all sufficiency in all things, may abound to every good work" (2 Corinthians 9:8)

Sin shall not have dominion over born-again child because he is not under the law, but under grace. By one man's disobedience many were made sinners and so by the obedience of one shall be many made righteous.

The righteousness does not confine to only many as few understand, but to all those who confess their sins to God and accept Jesus as their personal Savior.

The law pointed the guilt of a person but the salvation is through the grace by faith in Jesus Christ. In him alone is salvation and there is no other way for being with him for ever and ever.

Where sin abounded grace did much more abound and that is the reason why no matter how serious is the sin a man may have committed, except for blasphemy of the Holy Spirit, there is forgiveness in Jesus.

Sin brought death but grace from Jesus gives us eternal life. Jesus Christ is our Lord and he is faithful to forgive us our sins.

What shall we say then, should we continue in sin that grace may abound. Apostle Paul says "God forbid". We who are dead to sin will not live in sin any longer. We are baptized into Jesus Christ into his death. (Romans 5:19-21 and Romans 6:1-3)

Those who seek to do good works and earn salvation by their own works do nullify the importance of blood of Jesus Christ.

The blood of Jesus Christ that cleanses the sin has no value for them. They diligently keep doing good works in order to receive salvation neglecting the repeated emphasis from the Lord Jesus Christ that there is eternal life only in and through him.

As we read in 2 Corinthians 9:8 God is able to make grace abound to every good work. But good works are not the way for salvation.

The good works follow when a man is born-again. The blood of Jesus shed on the cross of Calvary can only save a person. This is the only way to receive eternal life. Salvation is available to all those who go to him and accept him as the Lord.

Now, here is the question: After having been delivered from the bondage of sin by grace through faith should a child of God keep sinning because he is under the grace but not under law?

No. Never should a child of God return to sin and lose blessings from God. Salvation is not lost for those who are saved in the blood of Jesus Christ; however, the Scripture does not endorse repeated sinning.

God will surely chide and chastise the one that falls repeatedly into sin and seeks grace time and again. Should we not consider the fact that if we yield to sin we are servants to sin; and sin becomes our master? We are under grace and we should remain servants to our Lord and be obedient to put on Christ as written in Ephesians 4:24.

We were, once servants of sin; but after accepting Jesus as our master, we have become servants of righteousness. We should bear fruit unto the Lord by leading a life of holiness and have assurance that there is everlasting life for us in eternity. The law has concluded all of us under sin, but the gift of God is eternal life through Lord Jesus Christ.

"And that ye put on the new man, which after God is created in righteousness and true holiness". (Ephesians 4:24)

CHAPTER 29
FEAR OF DEATH

"And deliver them who through fear of death were all their lifetime subject to bondage. For verily he took not on him the nature of angels; but he took on him the seed of Abraham" (Hebrews 2:15-16)

A strongly built man in his pomp and pride might feel great until the Lord interferes in his life to teach him lessons of obedience and reverence. No matter how healthy and wise one may be, yet the days of feeling nothingness in his life, and vanity of earthly life, come to his realization when he feels sick. The Lord can pull a nerve here and there to control any proud man. He has control over everyone's life and he hates pride but loves the humble.

God does not subject true Christians to troubles or trials or tests for no reason. Every test that he subjects us to has reason, and His invisible hand is always at work to lead us into successful Christian life.

We will come to know of His mysterious interference in our lives at the end of the test that we would have faced. God says that all things work for good to them that love Him and those who are called according to His purpose.

"And we know that all things work together for good to them that love God, to them who are the called according to his purpose. (Romans 8:28)

Everyone has to face death, a reality that we cannot thwart away. It is by one man's transgression of God's command that death entered into the world, and it is by one man's propitiation that we have life. Our everlasting life is not in anyone who was born man, or took the nature of angels, but in Lord Jesus Christ, who became man for our sake, even though He was divine.

"Wherefore, as by one man sin entered into the world, and death by sin; and so death passed upon all men, for that all have sinned" (Romans 5:12)

"For as by one man's disobedience many were made sinners, so by the obedience of one shall many be made righteous" (Romans 5:19)

The fellowship man had with Almighty God was lost and the LORD had to send His one and only Son into this world in the likeness of man to die for us and save unto everlasting life those that believe in Him.

Often it is seen that a believer fears the pain that he faces before dying rather than the death itself. We do not know exactly why God allows suffering during the last days of our life; but it is indeed a cause for much worry, as to who would look after us when we are old or lie on sick bed. It is that waiting for death that bothers much rather than the fear of death.

Every believer knows that at the other shore of his death there is pleasantness, and no pain, no cry, and yet human as we are, we do feel frustrated and disappointed some times.

It is in those times that we need comfort that God is there always with us. The shortest verse in the Bible is "Jesus wept" (John 11:35). Indeed Jesus took part in the suffering of parting of Lazarus from Mary and Martha and wept along with them.

It is therefore, we should know that there is no reason to be afraid of death. Lord Jesus Christ's body did not see corruption when He was in the grave. Because He was the Son of God and was fully obedient to the Father, He raised Him from the death.

The fear of dying in man is the result of either sickness or hopelessness. The fear and the hopelessness are the treasures of Satan, and it is because we do not fully depend on God we yield to the pressures of earning the treasures of Satan. The treasures of Satan include the feeling of darkness in life, and pessimism.

However, there is great hope for us that we will be in the presence of the light forever, and that light is Lord Jesus Christ. There is no other light needed in heaven except that of Lord Jesus Christ. He illuminates everything and there is no darkness in either Him or in heaven.

The heaven is our inheritance promised to us and the Lord fulfills His promise in us, and surely we will have happiness and joy reigning with Him in eternity.

"And I saw no temple therein: for the Lord God Almighty and the Lamb are the temple of it" (Revelation 21:22)

"And there shall be no night there; and they need no candle, neither light of the sun; for the Lord God giveth them light: and they shall reign for ever and ever" (Revelation 22:5)

The hope God gave us is that we are redeemed from the fear of death, which troubles man for a lifetime. He saved us and He will sustain us. He is in control of every situation in our lives. There is no reason to be missing that joy of Holy Spirit's presence in our hearts comforting us always.

Lord Jesus destroyed the power of death, and the devil that had control over the death. He did not take the nature of angels, but He took the nature of man.

The salvation and the hope of everlasting life are not only for Jews, but by their rejection of Lord Jesus Christ as their Messiah, it is for Gentiles as well. The seed of Abraham is in essence, not of physical descendants, but of all those who lived by faith in Him, and saved by grace through faith.

CHAPTER 30
THE BLESSED HOPE

"In a moment, in the twinkling of an eye, at the last trump: for the trumpet shall sound, and the dead shall be raised incorruptible, and we shall be changed" (1 Corinthians 15:52)

Jesus admonishes Martha reminding her that if she believed in Him she will see the glory of God. Then, they took away the stone from the place where Lazarus was laid to rest. Then Jesus lifted up His eyes and prayed to the Father.

In His prayer Jesus thanked the Father for hearing His prayer and said that the Father always hears Him. He prayed so in order that those who stood by Him may believe that the Father sent Him.

Jesus, after praying, cried out with a loud voice "Lazarus come forth". Notice Jesus called the dead man by his name; else, perhaps many dead would have come forth. The voice of Jesus was so powerful that the dead Lazarus rose to life and came forth. Another very noticeable fact is that the hands and feet of Lazarus were still bound with grave-clothes, and his face was bound with a napkin.

Comparison with the rising of the Lord Jesus Christ Himself, much later, when His hour was come, would show that the napkin that was bound on the face of Jesus was laid aside nicely folded, indicating that He Himself unloosened His bindings, and then folded the napkin that was bound on his head, and placed it at the side where His head was laid.

There was no assistance required for unloosening the wrap around the dead body of Jesus in the tomb. The tomb was covered with a stone, which was sealed and Jews made sure that no one stole His body.

There was no scope of spreading false rumors that He was not raised from the dead, and yet there are many, in some circles, in the present generation, spreading false rumors that He did not die on the cross, nor did He rise from the dead.

Indeed, Jesus died according to Scriptures, and there is evidence secular history as well. He appeared before many men, at different intervals, for forty days after His resurrection and before His ascension into heaven. He showed nail marks on his hands and feet to Thomas. He was the first-fruits.

Lord Jesus Christ commanded that Lazarus be unbound of the grave-clothes and the napkin that he may go. Thus, Lazarus was raised to life only to die again later because he was mortal, but Lord Jesus Christ was the Son of God, in the form of man, and therefore, His body did not see corruption in the grave and He rose in glorified body, which could pass closed doors, eat fish, appear and disappear at His will instantly at desired place.

It is the blessed hope of all believers in Christ that the dead will rise and receive glorified bodies, instantly, and those who are alive will follow them in similar glorified bodies, transformed at the twinkling of an eye, when they are "caught up" at the coming of Lord Jesus again. (Cf. 1 Thessalonians 4:16-17, and 1 Corinthians 15:52)

"For the Lord himself shall descend from heaven with a shout, with the voice of the archangel, and with the trump of God: and the dead in Christ shall rise first: Then we which are alive and remain shall be caught up together with them in the clouds, to meet the Lord in the air: and so shall we ever be with the Lord" (1 Thessalonians 4:16-17)

"But David said, 'You shall not do so, my brothers, with what the LORD has given us. He has preserved us and given into our hand the band that came against us. Who would listen to you in this matter? For as his share is who goes down into the battle, so shall his share be who stays by the baggage. They shall share alike.' And he made it a statute and a rule for Israel from that day forward to this day" (1 Samuel 30:23-25 ESV)

CHAPTER 31
BOLDNESS TO APPROACH
THE FATHER

The Church consisting of believers in Christ, irrespective of whether they are Jews or Gentiles, is given the privilege to know about the existence of principalities and powers.

"For we wrestle not against flesh and blood, but against principalities, against powers, against the rulers of the darkness of this world, against spiritual wickedness in high places. (Ephesians 6:12)

God loved all of us so much that according to his eternal purpose that he purposed in Jesus Christ He has let known this mystery and of the greatness of His creation to us who are the members of the Church.

The appreciation that a believer has about the creation of God and the blessings that God showered on the Gentiles on par with Jews, is greater than the wisdom that the world has ever known of the creation and the grace of God towards those who are in him.

Through Jesus Christ, our high priest, we have the boldness and courage to approach the Father. The tribulations that we face on this earth are for glory. Apostle Paul says he bowed his knees unto the Father of our Lord Jesus Christ.

Paul wrote the epistle to Ephesians as also to us through these scriptures that the believers do not need to be afraid of tribulations because they are meant to bring blessings and glory to us.

Paul desired that God may grant strength to the inner man by the Holy Spirit according to the riches of glory in God. Paul wanted us to allow Christ to dwell in our hearts that we may be rooted firmly in love. He desired that we may know the breadth, the length, the depth and the height of God's love towards us.

Unto him be glory in the church by Christ Jesus throughout all ages, world without end. Amen. (Ephesians 3:21)

"That the Gentiles should be fellowheirs, and of the same body, and partakers of his promise in Christ by the gospel" (Ephesians 3:6)

Whoever believes Jesus as Savior, irrespective of whether he is a Jew or Gentile, or male or female, will receive salvation. The death of Jesus on the cross, His burial and His resurrection is to be acknowledged by the one who seeks salvation.

"Having abolished in his flesh the enmity, even the law of commandments contained in ordinances; for to make in himself of twain one new man, so making peace" (Ephesians 2:15)

As Paul mentions the mystery of "One New Man" was hidden during the Old Testament period and it was revealed in the New Testament period.

"Of which salvation the prophets have enquired and searched diligently, who prophesied of the grace that should come unto you" (1 Peter 1:10)

Peter advises the dispersed Jews among Gentile nations, and Gentiles in those lands that they should gird up their loins of their minds, be vigilant, and hope to the end for the grace that was to be brought by Jesus at His second coming.

Peter emphasized that the salvation by grace through faith was not understood by not only Old Testament Saints, but even by the angels.

Peter quotes Old Testament verse (Leviticus 11:44), where the LORD God spoke to the children of Israel by the mouth of Moses and Aaron that they should sanctify themselves, and be holy because the LORD is holy.

The LORD God commanded them through Moses that they should not defile themselves by eating any kind of food that was prohibited by Him.

Later Apostle Paul writes, by the revelation of Jesus Christ, not to allow anyone to judge them in meat, or in drink, or in respect of any holiday, or the new moon, or of the Sabbath days, and thus legalism is done away with. (Colossians 2:16)

Peter advises the dispersed Jews among Gentile nations, and the Gentiles in those lands that they should keep away from the kind of lusts that they lived in, before they became disciples of Jesus. He said that even in their conversations with others they were to remain holy because God called them holy.

The spiritual man seeks spiritual things and fleshly man seeks fleshly pleasures.

While spiritual things bring blessings in one's life, fleshly things bring ruin. While gathering riches that are necessary for one's life is not sin, excessive gathering of riches out of greed, will bring ruin. Jesus said no man can serve two masters; either he will serve God or mammon (cf. Matthew 6:24, Matthew 19:24)

Every follower of Jesus Christ should know that the Father, whom they call on, is impartial in judging them of their work while they are on their journey to the eternal abode in heaven. We are sojourners on this earth and our inheritance is in heaven.

Therefore, seek only the things that are needed in heaven and gather for future residence, the treasures that last eternally than that of the things that perish. We are redeemed from the bondage of sin not with corruptible things, such as silver and gold, or from vain conversations received by tradition from predecessors, but with the precious blood of Jesus Christ, who was the Lamb of God, without any blemish and without any spot.

Lord Jesus said:

"Lay not up for yourselves treasures upon earth, where moth and rust doth corrupt, and where thieves break through and steal" (Matthew 6:19)

Lord Jesus Christ was chosen by the Father even before the foundation of the world that He should become the sacrificial Lamb of God, and accordingly He was on this earth and lived among us. He preached repentance, and the imminent "kingdom of heaven".

Jews rejected Jesus as their Messiah and, therefore, the establishment of literal kingdom was postponed, and the salvation was offered to the Gentiles as well. After the resurrection of Jesus from the dead,

Apostle Peter, and other apostles, as also Apostle Paul, who followed them preached the Gospel of Grace, which was salvation by Grace through faith; and it was the gift of God.

Peter asserts that the disciples of Jesus and those from Gentiles, who were converted, do believe in God, who raised Jesus from the dead. They all believe that the Father gave back the glory to Jesus, who had it when He was with the Father. He had relinquished it, when He came into the world in the form of a servant, and in the likeness of man.

When the glory of the Father was restored to the Son, He became the hope of all believers that they might have hope in Him. Peter's desire was that we all love one another fervently with a pure heart.

Those who believe in Jesus, and are born-again are saved, not by corruptible seed, but by incorruptible seed, by the word of God that lives and abides in them forever. The Lord and His will endure forever, while the grass withers and so do all flesh, and the entire glory of man perishes as does the flower of grass.

Heaven and earth shall pass away, but my words shall not pass away. (Matthew 24:35)

So shall my word be that goeth forth out of my mouth: it shall not return unto me void, but it shall accomplish that which I please, and it shall prosper in the thing whereto I sent it (Isaiah 55:11)

Peter and other disciples as also Apostle Paul preached this word of God. The word of God does not perish nor shall pass away; but endures forever.

The disciples preached the Gospel of Jesus Christ, whose blood cleanses us from all sin. Peter preached initially to Jews and later to Gentiles as well, as we read in Acts 10; whereas Paul was chosen by the Lord to preach primarily to the Gentiles (cf. Acts 9:15)

The Good News about the Gospel of Jesus Christ is about His death, burial and resurrection. He died on the cross, for our sake and on behalf of us, bearing our sin upon Him, in order that we may be delivered from our sin, and that we may receive everlasting life. The salvation is available for all those who confess sins and accept Him as Savior, and believes in heart that God raised Him from the dead (Cf. Romans 10:9)

Old Testament saints prophesied about our resurrection and had faith that they will see God.

"For I know that my redeemer liveth, and that he shall stand at the latter day upon the earth" Job 19:25
(Cf. Psalm 6:5; Psalm 16:10; Psalm 17:15; Psalm 30:3; Psalm 49:15; Psalm 73:24; Psalm 89:48)

Lord Jesus Christ, by rising from the grave showed us that we will not be left in the grave but rise from it to have everlasting life.

"But whosoever drinketh of the water that I shall give him shall never thirst; but the water that I shall give him shall be in him a well of water springing up into everlasting life" John 4:14

We are sealed with the Holy Spirit of Promise, and therefore, we should not grieve Holy Spirit by committing sins repeatedly.

"In whom ye also trusted, after that ye heard the word of truth, the gospel of your salvation: in whom also after that ye believed, ye were sealed with that holy Spirit of promise" Ephesians 1:13

"And grieve not the holy Spirit of God, whereby ye are sealed unto the day of redemption" Ephesians 4:30

Our salvation is secure and it will not be lost. Referring to those who are already saved by the precious blood of Jesus Christ, the Bible says that all of us were once enemies to God, and went astray like sheep, but then we are returned to the Shepherd by trusting Him as our shepherd.

God loved us first and had compassion on us and He, who forgave us of our sins, is not human to backslide on His promise to take back the gift He gave us, but He chastises us when we go astray. It is by hearing that faith comes, and the hearing by the word of God. (cf. 1 Peter 2:25, Romans 10:17)

"But God commendeth his love toward us, in that, while we were yet sinners, Christ died for us". (Romans Ch. 5:8)

It is the Father in heaven, who sent His only begotten Son Jesus, draws men to come to Him, and Lord Jesus Christ, to whom all power is given by the Father, will raise from the dead, them that believed in Him (cf. John 6:44)

Ephesians chapter 2:8-10 reveals a great truth that the gift of salvation cannot be gained by doing any amount of good works, but it is received only by grace through faith in Jesus.

None can boast that he or she received salvation by doing good works; however, a true believer would live to do good works after he has received salvation by grace through faith. We are His workmanship, and therefore, He does not tolerate any sin. Every sin is abominable to God, and no believer, who commits sins after receiving salvation, would escape chastisement.

Christ is the head of the Church, and those that have Lord Jesus Christ as their personal savior, are the members of the Church. The Church is His bride and the bride is the possession of Lord Jesus Christ.

When Lord Jesus Christ comes again the church is caught up to be with Him for ever and ever. He protects His treasured possession from the "great tribulation". Thus we are so privileged that our salvation is sealed with the Holy Spirit of promise, and no one can take away our salvation.

My Father, which gave them me, is greater than all; and no man is able to pluck them out of my Father's hand. (John 10:29)

www.ingramcontent.com/pod-product-compliance
Lightning Source LLC
Chambersburg PA
CBHW060511030426
42337CB00015B/1845